The Boy Allies with Uncle Sams Cruisers

Ensign Robert L. Drake

Contents

THE BOY ALLIES WITH UNCLE SAMS CRUISERS

BY

Ensign Robert L. Drake

THE BOY ALLIES WITH UNCLE SAMS CRUISERS

By Ensign Robert L. Drake

CHAPTER I
JACK'S ADVENTURE

Frank Chadwick jumped from a chair in the front window and ran toward the door. A form had swung from the sidewalk along the drive that marked the entrance to Lord Hasting's London home and at sight of it Frank had uttered an exclamation. Now, as the figure climbed the steps, Frank flung open the door.

"Jack!" he exclaimed with outstretched hand. "I feared something had happened, you have been gone so long and we had heard nothing of you."

"I'm perfectly whole," laughed Jack, grasping his friend's hand. "Why, I've been gone less than two weeks."

"But you expected to be gone only a day or two."

"That's true, but a fellow can't tell what is going to happen, you know. I wasn't sure I should find you here when I returned, though."

"You probably wouldn't had you come a day later," returned Frank.

"How's that?"

"We sail tomorrow night," said Frank.

"By George! Then I'm back just in time," declared Jack. "Where bound this time?"

"I don't know exactly, but personally I believe to America."

"Why?"

The United States, I understand, is about to declare war on Germany. I have heard it said that immediately thereafter American troops will be sent to Europe."

"What's that got to do with our voyage?"

"I'm coming to that. There will be need, of convoys for the American transports. I believe that is the work in which we will be engaged."

"That will be first rate, for a change," said Jack.

"But come," said Frank, leading the way into the house. "Where have you been? Tell me about yourself."

"Wait, until I get a breath," laughed Jack, making himself comfortable in a big armchair. "By the way, where is Lord Hastings?"

"He is in conference with the admiralty."

"And Lady Hastings?"

"Shopping, I believe. However, both will be back before long. Now let's have an account of your adventures."

"Well, they didn't amount to much," said Jack.

"Where've you been?"

"Pretty close to Heligoland."

"What! Again?"

"Exactly. You remember how Lord Hastings came to us one day and said that the admiralty had need of a single officer at that moment, and that we both volunteered?"

"I certainly do," declared Frank, "and we drew straws to see which of us should go. I lost."

"Exactly. Well, when I reached the admiralty I found there a certain Captain Ames. I made myself known and was straightway informed that I would do as well as another. Captain Ames was in command of the British destroyer Falcon. He was bound on active duty at once, and he took me along as second in command."

"Where was he bound?" demanded Frank. "And what was the nature of the work?"

"The nature of the work," said Jack, "was to search out German mines ahead of the battleships, who were to attempt a raid of Heligoland."

"Great Scott!" exclaimed Frank. "I hadn't heard anything about that. Was the raid a success?"

"It was not," replied Jack briefly.

"Explain," said Frank.

"I'm trying to," smiled Jack. "Give me a chance, will you?"

He became silent and mused for a few moments. Then he said meditatively:

"The destroyer service might well be called the cavalry of the sea. It calls for dashing initiative, aggressiveness and courage and daring to the point of rashness. Where an officer would be justified --even duty bound -- by navy standards to run away with a bigger and more valuable vessel, the commander of a destroyer often must close in to almost certain annihilation."

"Hm-m-m," said Frank slyly. "You are not feeling a bit proud of yourself, are you?"

"Oh, I'm not talking about myself," said Jack quietly. "I was thinking of a man like Captain Ames -- and other men of his caliber. However, I've been pretty close to death myself, and having come as close to a fellow as death did to me, I believe he'll become discouraged and quit. Yes, sir, I don't believe I shall ever die afloat."

"Don't be too cock-sure," said Frank dryly. "However, proceed."

"Well," Jack continued, "I followed Captain Ames aboard the Falcon and we put to sea immediately. It was the following night the, we found ourselves mixed up in the German mine fields and so close to the fortress itself that we were in range of the land batteries as well as the big guns of the German fleet. Our main fleet came far behind us, for the big ships, of course, would not venture in until we had made sure of the position of the mines."

"Right," said Frank. "I can see that -"

"Look here," said Jack, "who's telling this story?"

"You are," said Frank hastily. "Go ahead."

"All right, but don't interrupt me. As I said, we'd been searching mines for the battleships. Better to lose a dozen or two of us little fellows than one of the dread-noughts, so we steamed ahead like a fan with nets spread and a sharp lookout. We lost a few craft by bumping mines, but we destroyed a lot of the deadly things by firing into the fields and detonating them.

"We could generally tell when we were getting close to a field, which at this point was protected by the land batteries, for the batteries would redouble their fire. Might better have saved their powder and let us run into the fields and be blown to bits, you will say. Not at all. They would consider that a waste of good mines. Nobody wants to waste a whole mine on a poor little torpedo boat destroyer -- and twenty to forty men. There's no profit in that.

"We were sneaking along slowly, feeling our way and sitting on the slippery edge of eternity when the batteries opened up.

"'We're getting warmer,' said Ames.

"It was close range work and we were able to reply to the fire of the land batteries with our little 3-inch beauties, although I don't suppose we did much good. It makes a fellow feel better, however, as you know, if he's barking back. It's funny how most men have a dread of dying without letting the other fellow know why he's there. It doesn't seem so bad when you're hammering him.

"Anyway, it was part of our business.

"There was a bunch of red buoys anchored along one side where our chart showed the channel to be, and we supposed that they had been used by the German destroyers as channel buoys or to mark mine fields.

"It developed that the Germans had anchored those buoys and got the range of them so they could have their guns already set for anything that came near them. Some of our boats were hit by the first fire. It was a desperate spot.

"We were up near the lead and we had to run fairly well in advance of the main body. As you know, it often happens that when a vessel is steaming head-on very fast, it is difficult to hit her. It seems to rattle the gunners the same as charging infantry does the defenders.

"Shell after shell missed, but there were so many of them falling around us that we were almost smothered in the spray. We had all been under fire before, so it didn't have much effect on us, though.

"Then a shell hit us amidships and tore out one of our boilers. I was on the bridge with Captain Ames at the time.

"'Go below and report,' said Ames, just as calmly as though we were at maneuvers and one of our piston rods was pounding a little.

"I went down into a cloud of steam and found two men, pretty well scalded, dragging out the others who had been more badly hurt by the explosion. There wasn't enough of the water tight compartment left to shut it off from the rest of the vessel, but we still had one boiler intact.

"I directed the men to carry the wounded above and started back for the bridge. Just as my feet were on the bottom of the ladder there was another crash. The body of a man who had just reached the deck came toppling down in a shower of splinters and debris.

"Well, I got back on to my feet and made the deck. A shell had exploded right atop of us and nearly swept us clean. The bridge was almost carried away. Captain Ames lay under a light steel beam and I thought he was dead. I ran over to him. As I approached he shook off the beam and got up. One of his legs gave way and he had to hold on to a stanchion for support.

"'Cut off my trouser leg!' he shouted, very much excited.

"I ripped out my knife and did as he ordered. Then he twisted the cloth around his leg above an ugly gash and tied it.

"'What's gone below?' he demanded. 'One boiler,' I replied.

"'Might have been both,' grunted Ames, and added, 'Well, we're not out of this fight yet.'"

Jack paused a moment.

"A brave man!" cried Frank. "Go ahead, Jack."

Jack cleared his throat and proceeded.

CHAPTER II
THE BATTLE

"Well," Jack continued, "Ames espied one of the destroyers that had been leading us floundering around helplessly, with the German destroyer, which had appeared from nowhere, trying to cut her off.

"'Templeton,' said Ames, 'take the hand steering gear and run in there and get that fellow out.'

"I ran over to the hand gear. A fellow couldn't be frightened with a man like Ames telling him what to do. Ames propped himself up against what was left of the bridge and directed the gunners while we made the best speed we could with our single boiler.

"They were still dousing us with water, but the shells were not falling on board now. The two German destroyers were sweeping down on the helpless boat ahead, the missiles from their light guns playing a regular tattoo on her. It was an even chance we wouldn't find a live man aboard her.

"Ames was having a glorious time where he had propped himself against the shattered bridge. He swore every time one of our shells missed and he laughed gleefully every time one went home.

"We were only about a thousand yards from the British destroyer now and it looked like there was a fair chance of getting her out of the mess. I was beginning to have hope when I heard the screaming of a heavy shell from one of the land forts. Exactly amidships of the destroyer it landed. It broke her back and all her ribs, so to speak. Steam and steel and water and men flew high in the air. Everything aboard her was blown to bits.

"There was no use trying to tow her out now. I searched the water with my glass for living men. I figured we might be able to save a few if any survived, although it was against admiralty orders to stop when in danger. I didn't believe in the admiralty's stand at that moment. But I couldn't make out a living soul.

"The Germans immediately turned their attention to us. Their marksmanship was getting better. There was a frightful jar and the steering gear was wrenched out of my hands and I was thrown to the deck. When I picked myself up there was nothing with which to steer. Our rudder and a part of our stern had been shot away --

"'Alternate the screws!' Ames yelled. 'I'm busy with these guns. We'll fight as long as she floats!'

"The speaking tubes existed no longer. I stationed a man at the hatch -- and another below and transmitted my orders to the engine room by them. First we drove ahead with one screw, then with the other, to get a zig-zag course; next we backed first with one propeller and then the other. Each time we backed farther than we went forward, for I wanted to get out of the mess if possible. The crazy course threw the enemy gunners off somewhat.

"Suddenly I heard a yell from Ames. We'd put one of the German destroyers out of business. The other one was steaming toward us, but she was a long ways off,

"The men were cheering. I looked at the second destroyer, thinking we must have finished her, too, but she was still firing. Then I glanced around to see what the men were yelling about.

"Right into that hail of fire steamed a little mine sweeper. She looked for all the world like a tugboat. She had a single gun mounted in her bow, and one or two amidships. She had no armor and a rifle bullet probably would have pierced her sides with ease, but she pounded straight toward us; the water around her was beaten to a foam.

"Far out on the prow stood a man with a coil of rope. Ames sent a man to our stern. The sweeper had come close. The man in the prow swung his rope and let the coil fly. It fell across our stern. There wasn't much left to make it fast to, but we did it somehow and the sweeper started to tow us out of that particular part of the water.

"Our guns continued to bark at the destroyer, which was gaining on us. Some of our shots went home. The little old tugboat was hit once, but her master stuck to his task; and he undoubtedly saved our lives.

"Gradually we were pulled back, till at length we were under the protection of the guns of our fleet. From the flagship, signals were being flashed for our benefit. Ames read the flags through his glasses."

"'Congratulating us?' I asked.

"'Blast him, no!' shouted Ames. 'He wants to know why in blazes we didn't come out when we had a chance. Well, he wouldn't have come out himself had he been here, and I've been on the flagship, so we needn't feel sensitive about it!'

"And that's about all," Jack continued, "except for the fact that the raid by the battle fleet was given up. We cruised about for several days, in spite of our crippled condition. The ship's carpenter put us in condition to stay afloat, but at last we returned. I came here the moment I had landed."

"Well, you had a pretty strenuous time, if you ask me," declared Frank. "Too bad, though, that the raid couldn't have been made. We might have captured Heligoland."

"The Germans might capture Gibraltar," said Jack, with a vein of sarcasm in his voice, "but I don't think they will -- not right away."

"It can be done, though," declared Frank.

"What? The Germans capture Gibraltar?"

"No, I mean the British can take Heligoland. Wait until Uncle Sam gets in the war, he'll show you a few things."

"Maybe so," said Jack, "but what's all this talk I hear about the United States declaring war on Germany?"

"It's only talk, so far," said Frank, "but it seems certain to come. In fact, the war resolution already has passed the house and is being debated in the senate. It wouldn't surprise me if the senate passed it today. Then all that is needed is the signature of President Wilson."

"Well, let's hope there is no hitch," said Jack fervently.

"I don't think there will be. Come, let's go to our room and wait for Lord Hastings."

The two boys went upstairs, and while they are awaiting the arrival of Lord Hastings, a few words will be necessary to introduce them more fully.

Frank Chadwick was an American lad of possibly nineteen.

He had been in Italy when the great European war broke out, and through a misfortune had been shanghaied aboard a sailing vessel. After some adventures he fell in with Jack Templeton, a young Englishman, who had spent most of his life on the north coast of Africa. Together the lads had disposed of the crew of the vessel.

They became fast friends. Fortune threw them in the path of Lord Hastings, British nobleman and secret service agent, and they had gone through all kinds of troubles with him. Lord Hastings had commanded several vessels during the course of the war, and Jack and Frank upon these occasions had been his first officers.

Both lads spoke German and French fluently, and both had a smattering of several other tongues. Jack was huge in stature and of enormous strength for one of his age. Frank, on the other hand, was rather small, but what he lacked in physical strength he more than made up in courage.

Frank's greatest accomplishment, and one that had caused Jack much envy, was shooting. He could hit almost anything with a rifle, and revolvers in his hands were no less deadly.

Frank's chief trouble was his hot-headedness and more than once this had gotten him into such trouble that it took all Jack's resourcefulness to extricate him.

Both lads had seen service in many parts of the world since they had met Lord Hastings. Their commander recently had lost his vessel and the three had been on indefinite leave of absence.

The day before Jack's return Frank had been informed by Lord Hastings that they were about to put to sea again.

"Well," said Frank, when the two were in the room always reserved for their use when they were in London, "Lord Hastings will be glad to see you back again. He has been anxious, especially now that he has been ordered again on active service. He has been wondering where he would get a first officer."

"I guess you could, fill that place without any trouble," said Jack.

"I guess I could fill it all right, if I had to, but I would much rather have you along," declared Frank.

"Well, I'm glad to be back, old fellow," said Jack. "I'll admit that for a few minutes there the other night it looked as though I would never see London again, but everything is all right at last."

There were the sounds of footsteps below. These a few moments later ascended the stairs.

"Probably Lord Hastings," said Frank.

The lad was right and a moment later Lord Hastings stepped into the room. His eyes fell upon Jack and he advanced with outstretched hand.

"Jack!" he exclaimed. "I certainly am glad to see you again."

They shook hands heartily.

CHAPTER III
SAILING

"Frank tells me," said Jack, at the dinner table that evening, "that we are about to sail again; about to go into active service."

Lord Hastings smiled.

"There has been a slight alteration in plans since I spoke to Frank last," he said.

"You mean that we are not to go, Sir?" asked Frank. His face showed his disappointment.

"Not exactly," said Lord Hastings.

"But," Jack interrupted, "Frank said that we would help convoy American troops to England and France."

"Frank lets his imagination run away with him sometimes," said Lord Hastings quietly. "America has not yet declared war on Germany."

"But she will, sir," said Frank positively.

"That is probably true," said Lord Hastings, "although the resolution is being fought in the senate, according to latest cable advices. However, as you say, America will undoubtedly declare war. But even should American troops be sent to Europe it will not be for several months after war is declared."

"I thought they would send the regulars right away, sir," said Frank.

"Hardly. However, it is possible that an American fleet will be dispatched to act in conjunction with the British grand fleet in the war zone."

"Then we must sit home, sir?" asked Frank.

"I didn't say that," said Lord Hastings, smiling.

"You are too quick to jump at conclusions, Frank."

Frank flushed a trifle. "I'm just disappointed, sir," he replied.

"You need not be," said Lord Hastings. "There is work ahead. In fact, I may say that you will leave England some time tomorrow."

"Is that so, sir?" exclaimed Frank, happy again instantly. "Where do we go, sir?"

"I am not going at all," said Lord Hastings; "at least, not for some time yet. You and Jack will make this trip alone."

"That's too bad," declared Jack quietly. "We always like to have you with us, sir."

"I know you do," laughed Lord Hastings, "However, I will turn up later, so don't worry."

"In that event, it's all right," grinned Jack.

Will you, tell us where we are going, sir, and what we are to do?" asked Frank.

"I will if you will restrain your impatience," said Lord Hastings.

Frank felt this rebuke and became silent. A moment later Lord Hastings continued:

"I suppose you have heard that there is another German raider operating in the Atlantic off the coast of South America?"

"No, sir," said Frank, "I had not heard of it."

"Nor I," said Jack.

"Nevertheless, it's true," said Lord Hastings. Where it came from no one seems to know, but many merchant ships have been sunk by this raider. It is understood that she has citizens of allied countries aboard to the number of several hundred."

"Must be a big ship, sir," said Frank.

"So it is. It is probably a converted liner."

"Well, why haven't some of our cruisers picked it up, sir?" Jack wanted to know.

"They've tried hard enough," said Lord Hastings. "Trouble is this raider seems to have the heels of all ships of war. She simply runs away from them. However, the activities of the raider have become so serious that the government has decided she must be captured at all hazards."

"Which is where we come in," guessed Frank.

Lord Hastings gazed at the lad sternly.

"Frank," he said, "it's a wonder to me that your tongue hasn't got you into trouble long ago. Now, if you'll listen, I'll proceed."

Frank sat back abashed.

"Excuse me, sir," he said. "It won't happen again."

"All right, then," said Lord Hastings. "As I say, it seems impossible to come up with this raider by speed, so she must be captured or sunk by strategy. Now, I'll explain the plans to you, that you may know what to do and what will be expected of you."

Lord Hastings talked slowly for several hours, and the lads listened with unflagging interest. When His Lordship had finished it was almost midnight.

"Now, are you sure you understand?" he asked, getting to his feet.

"Perfectly, sir," was the reply.

"Very well, then, you had better turn in. You will sail aboard the Algonquin at five tomorrow evening. I will see that your reservations are made and that you are supplied with sufficient funds."

The lads went to bed.

When Jack and Frank went aboard the Algonquin the following evening half an hour before the sailing hour, they were dressed as civilians. Each wore a heavy traveling suit and overcoat and a steamer cap. Lord Hastings accompanied them aboard and introduced them to the captain, Stoneman by name, with whom His Lordship was well acquainted. Then Lord Hastings went ashore.

The Algonquin was an American vessel and sailed under American registry.

"I don't believe any raider will bother us," said Jack.

"Never can tell," declared Frank. "What's our destination, anyhow? I forgot to ask."

"Buenos Ayres," replied Jack.

"Wonder if there are many passengers aboard?"

"Doesn't look like it. We'll have a look at the passenger list."

They did so and found that the only passengers on the trip were two women, registered as Mrs. Silas Wheaton and Miss Elizabeth Wheaton.

"Looks like we would be pretty much to our ourselves," grinned Jack.

"So much the better," said Frank.

The Algonquin was not, in the true sense of the word, a passenger steamer. She had accommodations for some, but she was primarily a freighter, detoured this trip to carry a cargo of oil to the Argentine capital.

The vessel lifted anchor and steamed down the Thames promptly at 5 o'clock. At 6 the lads found themselves at dinner at the captain's table. There, too, they found Mrs. Wheaton and her daughter, Elizabeth. Introductions followed.

"I do hope we do not meet a submarine on the way," declared Miss Wheaton, who could not have been more than eighteen.

"I guess we are safe enough on that score," smiled Jack.

"Then they tell me there is a German raider operating off the coast of South America," said the girl. "We may be captured."

"Pooh!" exclaimed her mother. "Didn't I see guns front and back on this ship as I came abroad?"

"You mean fore and aft, mother," said the girl, smiling. "Yes, I saw the guns, too, but I don't imagine they would be much protection against a German raider."

"Then what are they there for?" Mrs. Wheaton wanted to know.

Jack and Frank laughed, and Captain Stoneman allowed a smile to wrinkle the corners of his mouth.

"Well, they won't dare attack us," said Mrs. Wheaton. "If they do the United States will make Germany pay for it."

"I guess Germany is not worrying about the United States right now," said Jack quietly.

"We'll make her worry," declared the woman.

"We're going to declare war and then the Kaiser will wish he had let us alone. Besides, there are probably American ships of war off the coast of South America. They will not allow us to be molested by a German raider."

"But, perhaps they won't be able to help it," mother, said the girl.

"Of course they will be able to help it," said the mother. "Now don't talk about this foolishness to me any more."

She arose and left the table. Her daughter followed her a few moments later.

"If the Germans get her they'll find they have caught a tartar," declared Jack.

"So they will," declared Captain Stoneman.

"By the way, Captain," said Frank, "do you fear the raider will attack us?"

"She will if she knows we are around," declared the captain grimly.

"And we are not prepared to fight her, sir?" asked Frank.

"Hardly," said the captain quietly.

"What's your crew?" demanded Jack.

"First, second and third officers, chief engineer, assistant and forty men," was the reply.

"And nothing worth while to shoot with," grinned Frank.

The captain brought his hand down hard upon the table.

"No!" he bellowed. "And still with these pirates sailing the seas, the American government won't allow us to carry guns big enough to do any damage."

"Well, we'll hope for the best," said Frank, rising.

The lads made their way on deck.

CHAPTER IV
THE RAIDER

Word of the United States' declaration of war upon Germany was flashed to the Algonquin on the fourth day out. It brought a thrill to Frank and to Captain Stoneman, an American himself.

Mrs. Wheaton, however, was the only person aboard who did any bragging as a result of it. She declared that now the United States had come to the rescue of the world, she had no fear of German raiders or Germans in any other shape or form.

The Algonquin was still two days out from Buenos Ayres. It was night. Came a hail from the lookout forward,

"Ship, sir!" he sang out.

"Where away?" demanded Captain Stoneman from the bridge.

"Dead ahead, sir!"

Half an hour later the light of an approaching vessel became visible to all on deck.

"The raider, do you suppose?" asked Frank, who stood near the captain.

"How do I know?" demanded the captain angrily. "It may be and it may not be."

A moment later the searchlight of the approaching vessel picked the Algonquin out of the darkness.

"Drat those searchlights!" shouted the angry captain. "If it wasn't for those things a man would have a chance."

The wireless operator hurried up.

"Message, sir," he exclaimed.

"Well, why don't you give it to me. What are you standing there for?"

"Vessel orders us to heave to or she'll put a shell into us, sir," said the operator, paying no attention to the captain's anger.

"She will, eh? What right has a bloodthirsty pirate like that to tell me what I can do? I won't do it."

Nevertheless Captain Stoneman gave the command to heave to.

"What's he sign himself?" he demanded of the wireless operator.

"He doesn't sign himself at all," was the reply.

"Drat him!" exclaimed the captain again. "Oh, well, we'll see what happens."

Half an hour later a small boat from the vessel that had accosted them scraped alongside the Algonquin.

"Throw over a ladder," came a voice in English. "I'm coming aboard you."

The captain of the Algonquin growled again but he gave the necessary order.

A moment later three figures scrambled on deck. At sight of the first man, Captain Stoneman's frown changed to a smile and he stepped quickly forward.

"Dash me if it isn't Lansing!" he exclaimed. "When did you get into the service, old man?"

The man in the uniform of a naval officer looked at the captain closely a moment, then extended a hand.

"Well, well, well!" he exclaimed. "If it isn't Stoneman. Where you bound, Captain?"

"Buenos Ayres. What ship are you?"

"American cruiser Pioneer, Stoneman. I'm the first officer."

"Good for you, son," exclaimed the captain. "First I took you for that German raider they say is sailing about in these parts."

"That's what I took you to be," declared the lieutenant. "I know there is no need searching your ship, Captain. You're true blue, but I'll have to have a look at your papers."

"Perfectly proper," said Captain Stoneman. "Come below."

The two disappeared below, but returned on deck a few moments later.

"Who are your passengers, Captain?" asked the American officer.

Captain Stoneman explained.

"Guess I'd better have a look at them anyhow, if it's no trouble," said the lieutenant.

"No trouble at all . Bo's'n," he called, "summon all passengers on deck."

Frank and Jack were already there, and approached. The American officer asked them a few questions, and then waved them away.

"All right," he said.

Mrs. Wheaton and her daughter appeared a few moments later. The former was angry. She approached the lieutenant.

"What do you mean by holding us up in this high-handed fashion?" she demanded.

"Necessity of war, madam," said the lieutenant with a bow.

"Necessity fiddlesticks," was the reply. "Who are you, anyhow?"

"I'm Lieutenant Lansing, American cruiser Pioneer, madam," came the reply.

Mrs. Wheaton's manner underwent an immediate change. "You'll pardon me, Lieutenant," she exclaimed. "Of course, I know you must do your duty."

After a few words with Mrs. Wheaton and her daughter, Lieutenant Lansing turned again to Captain Stoneman.

"All right, Captain," he said, "you may proceed. If leave you now just a word, though. Look out for that raider. She's around here some place. If you sight her, fire your guns, and if I'm within hearing I'll come up. Work your wireless, too. I'm here to nail that fellow."

"Very good," said Captain Stoneman. "You can count on me, Lansing."

The two men shook hands and the American naval officer, followed by his men, disappeared over the side. Captain Stoneman gave a signal and the Algonquin moved on again.

"Didn't take the United States very long to get started, did it?" said Frank, as they descended below.

"I should say not," was Jack's reply. "Still, I am afraid American cruisers will have no more success in nabbing the raider than have British vessels."

"Don't forget we're on the job," said Frank, with a smile.

"I'm not forgetting it," said Jack. "The sooner we come up with that fellow the better it will please me."

"Same here."

"Well, guess we may as well turn in," said Jack.

"Probably will be nothing doing tonight."

Five minutes later the lads were asleep.

Morning dawned clear and bright and Captain Stoneman congratulated himself that he was fast nearing his destination.

"Tomorrow morning at this time and we will be safe," he said at the breakfast table.

"Pooh," said Mrs. Wheaton. "What is there to be afraid of? Don't you know that the American cruiser Pioneer is in these waters?"

"But she is not in sight, mother," said her daughter.

"I'd like to know what difference that makes. Lieutenant Lansing knows that there are Americans aboard the Algonquin. He will not desert us."

"I am afraid," said Frank, "that Lieutenant Lansing has more important duties just now than seeing that the Algonquin reaches port safely."

"And what can be more important, I'd like to know?" demanded Mrs. Wheaton.

"Well, there are a whole lot of things," said Frank, "one of which is to nab this German raider, and I'll venture to say that the Pioneer is paying more attention to the raider right now than it is to the Algonquin."

"Young man," said Mrs. Wheaton, "it is perfectly plain to me that you do not know what you are talking about."

Frank flushed, and was about to reply. But he caught the eye of Miss Wheaton and remained silent. A few moments later he excused himself and left the table.

Fifteen minutes later Elizabeth Wheaton approached him on deck.

"Don't mind mother," she said with a smile. "It is just her way. She means no harm."

"Probably not," agreed Frank with a smile, "but you will admit that it is rather annoying."

Before the girl could reply, there came a hail from the lookout forward.

"Ship, sir!"

"Where away?" called the first officer, who held the bridge.

"Dead ahead!" came the reply.

Indeed, a ship was plainly visible to all on deck at that moment.

It came to the first officer in a flash that this vessel bearing down on the Algonquin was in all probability the German raider.

He summoned the captain.

Captain Stoneman came jumping on deck.

He gave one look at the approaching vessel, and then cried angrily, forgetting his grammar absolutely as he did so. "That's her! That's her as sure as I'm a foot high."

CHAPTER V
ABOARD THE RAIDER

Captain Stoneman now became the man of action that Jack and Frank knew he could be.

"Mr. Bronson!" he summoned the first officer, who approached hastily. "Mr. Bronson," continued the captain, "you point that gun aft toward the heavens and you fire it until I tell you to stop. Mr. Taylor, you do the same with the gun forward."

The captain glanced around. His third officer was busy. He called to Jack.

"Mr. Templeton," he cried, "you go below and tell my wireless operator to pick up the cruiser Pioneer. You tell him I said not to stop trying, or I'll be down and attend to him myself."

Jack hurried away to obey the command.

Frank approached Captain Stoneman.

"Can I be of any assistance, sir?" he asked.

The captain glared at him angrily. "No," he shouted; then added: "Yes. You stand at the hatchway there and don't you let either of those women come on deck. If you do, I'll toss you overboard."

Frank went to his post.

So far there had been nothing to indicate that the approaching ship was other than a peaceful vessel. She had, so far as Captain Stoneman knew, made no effort to pick up the Algonquin with her wireless.

"I wonder," said Captain Stoneman to himself, "whether that pirate is going to blow me up without warning, or whether that wireless operator of mine has gone to bed? I'll go down and find out."

He ordered his first officer away from the gun aft to take the bridge and ran below to the wireless room.

"Any message from the ship ahead?" he demanded.

"No, sir," was the operator's reply.

"What's all that 'click-clicking' about?"

"I'm trying to pick up the Pioneer, sir."

"Humph! Can't you raise her?"

"No, sir."

Captain Stoneman returned on deck without further words. He relieved the first officer and ordered him back to the gun aft. At almost the same moment, the forward gun, pointed high, spoke.

"That'll raise the Pioneer if she's around here," said Captain Stoneman aloud.

The aft gun also spoke now, and then both boomed again.

An instant later a cloud of smoke burst from the approaching vessel, followed by a heavy boom. A solid shot passed over the Algonquin and splashed in the water beyond.

"Humph!" said Captain Stoneman again. "Signal to heave to, eh? Well, I can't afford to disregard it."

He signaled the engine room and the Algonquin a few moments later came to a stop.

"Now, come on, you pirates," mumbled Captain Stoneman. "Come on aboard and tell me what you want."

A boat put off from the raider, for such the strange vessel proved to be. It came toward the Algonquin rapidly.

Captain Stoneman motioned to Frank.

"Better let the women come up now," he said quietly, "and Mr. Bronson, pipe all hands from below."

Before the small boat reached the Algonquin's side, all passengers and members of the crew were on deck. Frank pressed close to Jack.

"Got your gun?" he asked.

"In my boot," was the quiet reply; "and yours?"

"All right. How about your little decoration?"

Jack took a small object from his pocket and put it in the left-hand button hole of his coat. Frank followed his example.

"What is the meaning of this outrage?" demanded Mrs. Wheaton, as she watched the small boat approach.

"Meaning is that we are prisoners of the German raider," answered Captain Stoneman, who overheard the remark.

"And why?" demanded the woman. "I heard guns fired above here. Couldn't you hit anything?"

"We didn't try, madam," said the captain. "We fired those guns to notify the Pioneer we had encountered the raider."

"Well, why didn't you shoot at her?" demanded Mrs. Wheaton.

Captain Stoneman was about to make an angry retort, but restrained himself with a visible effort.

The raider's boat scraped alongside the Algonquin.

"Throw down a ladder here," said a voice in English, though with a heavy German accent.

Captain Stoneman growled ominously, but he ordered the command obeyed. A moment later a German naval officer appeared on deck. He was closely followed by half a dozen other figures. The officer approached Captain Stoneman.

"You are the commander of this vessel?" he asked.

"I am," was the reply. "What of it?"

"You'd best keep a civil tongue in your head," said the German. "What's your destination, and the nature of your cargo?"

"Buenos Ayres; oil," growled the captain, answering both questions briefly.

"Good!" said the German. "We are in need of oil." He turned to one of his men. "Below with you," he said. "Take three men and unloosen a hundred barrels of oil. I'll send a boat after them."

The man saluted and went below, followed by several of his companions. The German officer turned again to Captain Stoneman.

"You and your men, and these two ladies," he indicated Mrs. Wheaton and her daughter, "will be prisoners aboard the Vaterland. Captain Koenig will make you as comfortable as possible."

"Thanks," said Captain Stoneman briefly." I know enough about you Germans and what to expect."

"Silence!" thundered the German, "or I shall have you placed in irons."

Captain Stoneman shrugged his shoulders, but he held his tongue.

Now, for the first time, the German officer appeared to notice that Jack and Frank were not members of the Algonquin crew. He motioned them to approach.

"You are passengers?" he asked.

"Yes, sir," said Jack.

The German took a quick step forward as he noticed the little emblem on Jack's coat. He glanced at Frank and saw one there, too. He tapped the one that Jack wore with his finger.

"Where did you get that?" he asked sharply.

"Where could I get it but in one place?" was Jack's reply.

"You are no German," said the officer.

"I was not born in Germany, it is true," said Jack, "but my ancestors were. I am what some people are pleased to call a German-American."

"Good!" exclaimed the German officer. "But what are you doing here?"

"That," said Jack, "is rather a long story and one that I am commanded to tell to Captain Koenig."

The German officer hesitated.

"You come together?" he asked at length, indicating Frank.

"Yes," said Jack.

"Well," said the German, "you will realize that I must be careful. I must see if you are armed."

He examined the lads' clothing carefully.

"You will follow me," he said a few moments later.

The crew of the Algonquin, meantime, was being transferred to the Vaterland. Jack and Frank found themselves in the last boatload to go.

Aboard the Vaterland, as the two lads followed their captor to the cabin of the German commander, Frank saw the disgust in the eyes of Elizabeth Wheaton as he passed her. It was plain that she, at least, took him for what he represented himself to be to the German officer.

"Oh, well," said the lad, as he walked along, "it cannot be helped."

Captain Koenig asked the lads several sharp questions which apparently satisfied him that they were what they claimed to be.

"But I cannot land you yet," he said.

"Any time within the month will do, Captain," said Jack. "We still have a little time. We do not need to reach New York until two days before the meeting. You can set us ashore some place in time enough for us to get there."

"I'll do better than that," said the captain. "I'll set you ashore on the coast of

Florida three weeks from today."

"Good!" said Jack.

"Now," said the captain, "if you care to accompany me on deck, you shall see the last of the ship that carried you here."

The lads followed the captain on deck. The latter summoned his first officer.

"Fuses all set?" he asked.

"Yes, sir. The explosion should occur within one minute."

All turned their eyes to the abandoned Alqonquin.

Suddenly there was a terrible explosion. A sheet of flame sprang from the doomed vessel. She seemed to leap high in the sky, then settled down in two pieces. A moment later she disappeared from sight.

"You shall pay for that, Captain Koenig!" said Jack to himself, between clenched teeth.

CHAPTER VI
RECONNOITERING

Jack and Frank leaned against the lifelines, gazing over the stem of the Vaterland as the vessel's triple screws drove her ahead. Jack's eyes were fixed thoughtfully upon the strong if crudely constructed turret on the after deck, from which protruded the glistening nose of an 8-inch gun. His gaze wandered forward past the rakish stacks to the light bridge which spanned the Vaterland's beam. Mounted on the bridge, in addition to the two naval telescopes, were four rapid-fire guns, each capable of spitting bullets at the rate of five hundred a minute, though, sheltered as they were under the tarpaulins, they looked harmless enough.

Frank regarded Jack curiously.

"What's on your mind?" he asked.

"I was thinking," said Jack slowly, "that if I could get my hands on one of those machine guns on the bridge, these Germans would wish they were home in the Kiel Canal."

"You mean?" said Frank.

"I mean that if I had five minutes to man one of those rapid-firers up yonder I could rake this ship from stem to stern. There'd be a few less Germans in this world before they got me. Anyway, it's a point worth remembering."

Frank nodded his head.

"It certainly is," he replied.

Jack resumed his study of the big ship.

Half way up each mast he saw the round-covered dots which denoted the powerful searchlights, and from the tops of the thin masts sagged the wireless aerials. Immediately under the bridge and sheltered somewhat by it was the wireless room. The entire ship, even to the rifle barrels, was painted the dead, neutral gray which is known as "war color."

Frank followed the direction of Jack's gaze.

"They are well prepared, aren't they?" he said.

"They certainly are," declared Jack.

"Well," said Frank, "we must remember that we are to do nothing yet. The time will come, though, and it is as well to know beforehand what we will have to contend with."

"Exactly," said Jack. "That's why I am trying to impress all these things on my memory."

"Come," said Frank, "we'll interview the captain."

Jack followed his friend to the captain's cabin. The captain expressed much pleasure at seeing them.

"How goes everything this morning, Captain?" asked Frank.

"Good!" was the response. "What can I do for you?"

"We've just been looking about the Vaterland," said Jack in German. "It must have required remarkable ingenuity to have converted this ship into the formidable vessel it is now."

"You think so?" said the captain. "I am glad. I did it under my own plans."

"And you have had the most remarkable success," said Frank. "The Emperor will have much to thank you for when the war is over."

"Ja!" exclaimed Captain Koenig. "I shall have the Iron Cross."

"Undoubtedly, Captain," declared Jack. "By the way, how large a crew do you carry?"

"Almost two hundred officers and men," was the reply.

"But your prisoners," exclaimed Frank. "Surely you have many of them?"

"We have now more than 300 prisoners aboard this ship," declared Captain Koenig; "mostly men. Besides the women who came aboard with you, there are only five."

"That's a pretty big load, Captain?"

"The Vaterland," said Captain Koenig proudly, "has accommodations for more than a thousand souls."

"I knew it was a big ship," said Frank, "but I had no idea it carried so many. By the way, where do you keep your prisoners?"

"Forward, beneath the main deck," replied the Captain.

"They are well guarded, of course?"

"Well guarded, indeed," was the captain's reply.

"They are of course, unarmed and the door to their prison is locked. Besides, there are armed men on guard without every instant."

"I see you, have spared no pains to keep everything safe," said Frank.

"You are right, sir. The Vaterland is in my hands, and it shall stay in my hands. No ship of war can catch me. I am well prepared on all sides."

"Your foresight is to be commended, Captain," declared Jack. "The Kaiser has reason to be proud of you."

"You think so?" exclaimed Captain Koenig. "I am pleased."

The lads went on deck again after some further conversation.

"He's a pretty conceited old pirate, if you ask me," declared Jack.

"So he is," Frank agreed; "yet when you stop to think of it he has some reason to be. He's doing a pretty good job for the Kaiser."

"A pretty bad job for the Allies," said Jack.

"Which is the reason we are here," declared Frank. "Hello, here comes Miss Wheaton; I'll have a word with her."

He lifted his cap as he spoke. Miss Wheaton bowed and would have passed on had not Frank intercepted her.

"Won't you stop a moment, Miss Wheaton?" the lad asked.

"I wish to have nothing to do with German spies," returned the girl coldly.

"I beg your pardon," said Frank, and stepped back.

The girl passed on. Five paces beyond, however, she stopped, turned and retraced her steps.

"I had taken you for Americans, aboard the Algonquin," she declared. "Surely you are not German?"

"No," said Frank, "I am an American."

"And are helping the enemies of your country," declared the girl.

"Just a moment, Miss Wheaton," said Frank quietly. He looked around hurriedly. There was not a soul near, save Jack. "Do not believe all you see," the lad whispered.

"You mean?" exclaimed the girl.

Frank shrugged his shoulders. "Appearances are often deceitful," he said quietly.

Miss Wheaton looked at the lad in some amazement. Then she said: "I hope I do not misunderstand you."

"I am sure you don't," said Frank with a smile. "The Vaterland has been engaged in her nefarious trade altogether too long. It is time somebody put a stop to it. Well, the time will come."

Miss Wheaton extended a hand, which the lad grasped.

"I am sorry I doubted you," she said.

"Why, that's all right," said Frank.

The girl inclined her head and passed on. Framl turned to Jack.

"A very nice girl," he said, indicating Miss Wheaton.

"Most likely," Jack agreed. "However, you always were rather strong for the girls. I hope you didn't tell her our business."

"Why -- why, no," said Frank, flushing." I simply told her she must not believe all she sees."

"Which was simply another way of telling her we are not what we represented ourselves to Captain Koenig," said Jack. "Now she'll probably go straight to the captain and tell him what she has learned."

"No, she won't," said Frank. "She wouldn't do that."

"How do you know she won't?"

"Well, I don't know it, but I don't think she will."

"What you think and what she may do are likely to be altogether different," declared Jack. "You are too quick with your tongue sometimes, Frank."

"But," Frank protested, "she thought we were Germans and ignored us."

"What do we care what she thinks? If she ignores us so much the better to my way of thinking."

"But -" Frank began.

"But, nothing," interrupted Jack. "We are here for a single purpose, and it makes no difference what any one thinks of us."

"You are probably right, Jack," Frank agreed. "I'll have to keep a tight rein on my tongue. However, I am sure Miss Wheaton will not betray us."

"Humph!" said Jack, and the conversation ended.

It was late that afternoon when the lookout forward gave the news that there was a ship in the offing. Immediately the Vaterland altered her course slightly and headed for the newcomer, which it developed was a merchant ship.

"Here comes another victim," said Frank.

"You don't suppose --" began Jack.

"Too soon, I'm afraid," said Frank, with a shake of his head. "I wish it were, but I am afraid it is too soon."

Within range, the Vaterland put a shot across the bow of the stranger. The newcomer obeyed this command instantly.

She hove to.

CHAPTER VII
ABOARD THE STRANGER

It was the steamer Gloucester that the Vaterland had sighted and which had heaved to in response to the Vaterland's shot across her bow. The Gloucester was a small steamer, more on the order of a pleasure yacht than a freight vessel.

In one of the cabins, as the vessel came to, sat a man in an invalid chair. Beside him stood a huge negro.

"See what the trouble is, Tom," ordered the invalid as the ship's engines stopped.

The negro hurried on deck, but was back in a few minutes, breathing excitedly.

"It's the raider, suh," he said. "The Vaterland."

"Good!" said the man in the invalid's chair. "Wheel me on deck, Tom."

The negro did as ordered. There the invalid passed the word for the captain, who came toward him.

"Yes, sir," said Captain Tucker, saluting.

"The vessel ahead, I understand," said the invalid, "is the Vaterland?"

"It is, Mr. Hamilton."

"Very good. Call the first, second and third officers."

The captain obeyed and a few moments later the three officers stood before Hamilton.

"You must not forget, gentlemen," said 'Hamilton, "that we are bound simply on a pleasure cruise. I was not willing that a German raider should interfere with the prescription of an ocean voyage ordered by, my physician. You understand?"

The officers nodded.

The men were: First officer, Mr. Sanborn; second officer, Mr. Partridge, and third officer, Mr. Richardson.

"Very well, then," said Mr. Hamilton. "That is all."

He turned again to the negro. "Tom," he said, "bring my bags and stow them in the cutter yonder. We will be taken prisoners aboard the raider."

The negro did as commanded and again took his stand by Hamilton. "Mind, Tom," said Mr. Hamilton, "no weapons."

"None, suh?" questioned the negro.

"Not a single one."

"Well, suh," said the negro, "dis ain't no weapon I got here. I just carry it for luck, Mistah Hamilton."

He displayed a pair of brass knuckles.

"Very well," said Mr. Hamilton, "but be sure you put them where they will not be found."

"Dey won't find 'em," chuckled the negro.

He rolled up the leg of one trouser and stowed the brass knuckles carefully in the top of his sock.

As the Vaterland's small boat approached the Gloucester, Captain Tucker ordered a gangway rigged. Mr. Hamilton's chair was wheeled to this gangway, and those aboard waited the arrival of the German officer in the small boat.

Lieutenant Blum, the Vaterland's officer, leaped nimbly over the rail.

"The captain?" he demanded.

Captain Tucker stepped forward. "I'm Captain Tucker," he said. "This," he indicated Mr. Hamilton, "is the owner, Mr. Hamilton, who is on a voyage for his health."

"I'm sorry his health cannot be given more consideration," said Lieutenant Blum, "but I am under necessity of sinking your ship. Mr. Hamilton may continue his voyage aboard the Vaterland."

The prisoners were safely transferred to the Vaterland and a short time later a rumbling explosion marked the end of the steamer Gloucester.

Mr. Hamilton, through the courtesy of Captain Koenig, was assigned one of the larger cabins, near the captain's own. Hamilton spoke to Captain Koenig in fluent German. The German captain seemed to take considerable interest in the invalid.

As the chair of the invalid was wheeled along the deck, the invalid glanced sharply at Jack and Frank. Neither lad manifested the slightest surprise and Mr. Hamilton was soon out of sight.

Members of the crew of the Gloucester, all except the negro Torn, who was to be allowed to tend Mr. Hamilton personally, were soon locked safely between decks and the Vaterland proceeded on her way.

Several hours later, Captain Koenig, in paying a visit to the cabin found the latter studying over a chess board.

"Ha!" exclaimed Captain Koenig. "So you play chess, eh?"

"A little," said Mr. Hamilton.

"That is fortunate," declared the captain. "I too love the game. I shall be pleased to have you play with me at some future time."

"I shall be glad, Captain," said Mr. Hamilton quietly.

The German commander soon took his leave. Hamilton turned to the negro, who, upon the captain's departure, had taken the brass knuckles from his sock and was examining them carefully.

"Tom," said he, "if you don't keep those knuckles out of sight I shall heave them overboard."

"Yussuh," exclaimed Tom, and hid the knuckles hastily.

"Listen to me, Tom," said Hamilton. "Whenever I am in here I want you to station yourself outside the door. And I want you to tell me before you let any one in, understand?"

"Yussuh."

"And mind you keep those knuckles out of sight. There'll be no use for them until I give the word. Remember that."

"Yussuh."

There came a knock on the door and Hamilton fell back on his cushions as he ordered Tom to open the door. A moment later girl introduced herself and then said:

"I've come to see you because we are fellow prisoners, Mr. Hamilton, and to see if there is anything I can do for you. I know you cannot help yourself, being an invalid."

Mr. Hamilton smiled.

"Don't you worry about me, young woman," he said. "I'm not half so helpless as you think. See?"

Mr. Hamilton stood up, dropped the robe from his lap and skipped nimbly across the cabin.

Elizabeth Wheaton stepped back in surprise.

"But I thought -" she began.

"So does Captain Koenig," said Hamilton with a smile. "By the way, Miss Wheaton, are you armed?"

"No."

Hamilton explored the seat of his chair. He produced a box, which he opened. There lay at least a dozen shining automatics. Hamilton gave one to the girl.

"Take this," he said simply. "You may have need of it, although if nothing goes wrong with my plans, all will be well."

The girl took the weapon and hid it in the folds of her dress. At that moment Tom poked his head in the door indicating that some one was approaching. Miss Wheaton left the cabin without another word.

A moment later Jack and Frank entered the cabin. Mr. Hamilton, who was again in his invalid chair covered with a robe, leaped to his feet and extended a hand to each lad.

"By Jove! We are glad to see you, sir," said Frank, "although we did not expect you so soon."

"I started sooner than I had expected," laughed Lord Hastings, for such Mr. Hamilton proved to be. "Have you found out the lay of the land?"

"Yes, sir," replied Jack, and explained briefly. He produced a long sheet of paper, which he passed to Lord Hastings.

"What's this?" demanded the latter.

"Deck plan, sir," said Jack quietly. "I obtained it from Captain Koenig, sir, though he doesn't know it."

"Very good," said Lord Hastings, and examined it carefully.

Jack put a finger to the paper.

"There," he pointed out, "is the second deck. In here are the prisoners of the Algonquin and the Gloucester. In the compartment below are perhaps two hundred other prisoners. Abaft this compartment is the strong room in which are the small arms and ammunition. Lieutenant Blum carries the keys. In there, too, are hundreds of rifles."

"Very well," said Lord Hastings, and briefly sketched a plan of action. Then he added:

"This work must be done promptly and there must be no slip. A slip means failure. Now follow the instructions I give you."

He spoke softly for perhaps fifteen minutes, and when Frank and Jack took their leave at the expiration of that period, the faces of both were flushed.

"At 11 o'clock tomorrow morning," Jack whispered.

"Be a sailor," Frank instructed. "You mean six bells."

"All right," laughed Jack. "Have it your own way. Six bells or 11 o'clock. We'll be ready."

CHAPTER VIII
SIX BELLS

It was at 10 o'clock the following morning that Lord Hastings received a call from Captain Koenig.

"Ah!" exclaimed the German commander. "I find that I have time on my hands. Would it be too much to ask you to have a game of chess with me now?"

"Indeed, no," was Lord Hastings' reply. "I shall be pleased. I shall have my man roll me to your quarters within fifteen minutes."

"Very good!" said Captain Koenig. He bowed and departed.

Lord Hastings quickly ordered the negro to find Frank and Jack and order them to his cabin. A few moments more and they stood before him.

"Frank," said Lord Hastings, "you approach the bridge and stand there. When the men come from below, it may be that we will need a man near the bridge to pick off the gunner should he train one of the rapid-firers on us. Do not move, however, unless it is necessary. If we can reach the bridge without attracting attention by firing a shot it will be infinitely better. Jack, you come with me. I shall now engage the captain in a game of chess."

Frank stooped and from his boots brought out two automatics. Jack did likewise. These they put in their pockets. Then Frank left his commander's cabin.

Above he encountered Miss Wheaton, who approached him.

"I have learned what is about to happen," said the girl, "and I want to know if I can be of some assistance."

"You can help most," said Frank, "by going to your cabin and staying there. Make sure that none of the women come on deck."

"But," said the girl, "I had hoped to be of more value than that."

"Believe me," said Frank, "if you can make sure that the women remain in their cabins you will have done much."

Elizabeth Wheaton nodded her head. "None shall come out," she said quietly. She turned on her heel and made her way to her own cabin. Then she summoned the other women prisoners and when they were inside she locked the door, taking care, however, that none saw her turn the key, for she did not wish to answer unnecessary questions.

Frank took a position where he could cover the bridge. There were only two men there -- the officer of the deck and the quartermaster at the wheel.

Below, Lord Hastings motioned to the giant negro to wheel him to Captain Koenig's cabin.

"I'm depending on you, Tom," he said quietly. "When I give the word --"

"Yussuh!" said Tom, grinning. "I'll be watching you, suh."

He wheeled Lord Hastings to Captain Koenig's cabin. Jack followed.

The German commander expressed his pleasure at the opportunity of matching his wits against his prisoner across the chess board. He espied Jack and eyed him askance.

"I'm somewhat of a chess player myself," Jack explained. "I thought I would enjoy the battle. Mr. Hamilton, here, has no objections to my presence."

"Nor have I, in that event," said Captain Koenig.

The chess board stood upon a small table. The pieces were in place. Johnson wheeled Lord Hastings into position and fell into position behind him. Captain Koenig drew up a chair. Jack remained standing.

The ad was perfectly calm in spite of the excitement that raged in his breast. Lord Hastings played silently and without anxiety, as though nothing were about to transpire. Even the negro, Tom, showed nothing of the excitement that he felt. Now and then, though, his hand touched the pair of brass knuckles which he had transferred from his sock to his right-hand pocket.

As the game progressed Captain Koenig became manifestly pleased, for he felt that he was winning. Lord Hastings glanced at the clock. It lacked five minutes to 11. He looked at Tom significantly, and the negro shifted his position closer to Captain Koenig.

Suddenly six bells struck.

As the last stroke sounded, Lord Hastings, apparently accidentally, brushed one of the chessmen from the board.

"Your pardon," he said to Captain Koenig.

He bent over, apparently to pick up the chessman. Instead, his hand sought the box in his chair and when he sat straight again, his revolver covered Captain Koenig.

The commander of the Vaterland started up with an inarticulate cry. At the same moment Tom sprang forward, and his two hands grasped the German commander's throat.

Captain Koenig was fat and he was conceited and he had been foolishly lax. But he was a competent commander in the German navy, which means that he was a brave and resourceful man. He allowed his body to relax in the negro's clutch.

His foot sought for and found a tiny button below the chess table. He pressed it.

A buzzer sounded in another cabin.

The men in the cabin worked with swift and silent precision.

In answer to the pressing of the button there came a knock at the door. A moment later Lieutenant Blum entered. He took in the situation at a glance. Tom released his hold upon Captain Koenig and jumped for the lieutenant. As the negro's arms went round the man, Jack dipped quickly into the lieutenant's pocket and produced the keys to the quarters occupied by the prisoners, and to the store room.

The lieutenant writhed in the negro's grasp and with a kick caught Tom on the right shin. Immediately Tom released his bold and sought his brass knuckles. Before he could strike, however, Lieutenant Blum had disappeared through the door.

Jack whipped out his revolver and fired, but the German did not stop. The lad muttered an imprecation.

"Quick, now!" ordered Lord Hastings.

He was calm, cool and collected. Revolvers in the box were disposed of between the three, and then all dashed below to where the prisoners were locked.

Two men guarded the deck at this point. Seeing their enemies bearing down on them, both opened fire. The revolvers of Lord Hastings flashed simultaneously and the two Germans dropped.

Quickly Jack fitted one of the keys to the door, and the crews of the Algonquin and the Gloucester streamed forth. The first man out was Captain Stoneman. Jack gave him a pair of revolvers. The other weapons were divided up as far as they would go.

"To the bridge with you, Stoneman!" cried Lord Hastings. "You'll find Chadwick there. Take the bridge and hold those machine guns until we get there. Much depends on your getting there before the enemy can recover from their surprise." Stoneman dashed away. Lord Hastings designated that the others who were armed should follow. These hurried after Stoneman.

"Now for the rifles!" cried Lord Hastings.

Jack led the way and Lord Hastings and members of the Algonquin and Gloucester crews followed.

At the same moment a bugle blared above and there came the hoarse sounds of commands.

"We've been discovered!" shouted Jack.

"There is no time to lose, sir."

He fitted a key to the door of the compartment where the rifles, ammunition and small arms were stored. The men, perhaps sixty all told, rushed forward and grabbed weapons and ammunition.

"I'll lead these men, Jack," said Lord Hastings.

"One of those keys fits the other prisoners' compartment. Go below and release them. Arm them and then come on deck. You go with him, Tom. If any of the prisoners hang back, lock them up or shoot them. This is no time for fooling. You other men, follow me."

Lord Hastings dashed on deck, closely followed by his men.

Jack wasted no time. Quickly he descended to the deck below where the other prisoners were held. These, too, were under guard from the outside. Sounds of confusion from within told the lads that the prisoners had heard the sounds of firing above. Men kicked upon the barred door. They were eager to get out and join in the fray, the nature of which they could not tell.

The two Germans on guard there were plainly uneasy. No orders had reached them, and they appeared afraid that the door would give beneath kicks and blows rained upon it from within; and they knew that there would be no stopping the prisoners should they break through.

Consequently they were watching the door when lack and the negro appeared in sight and the attackers had the advantage. One swerved suddenly, however, and raised his weapon. Jack fired and the man dropped.

Tom accounted for the second. Then Jack opened the door. He held up a hand as the men streamed forth.

"Follow me and get guns!" he shouted to make himself heard above the babel of voices.

The others understood the import of the words. There was a wild cheer as they dashed after Jack and the negro Tom.

CHAPTER IX
THE FIGHT

Frank, on deck, was doing his work. At the first stroke of six bells, the lad had dropped his hand to his pocket. A moment later there came a sharp report from below.

"Things have started moving," said Frank quietly.

The officer on the bridge had also caught the sound of the revolver shot. He looked up sharply. A moment later Lieutenant Blum dashed forward and jumped to the bridge. He spoke hurriedly to the officer of the deck, and both made a leap for the machine guns.

Frank smiled quietly to himself. Here was fighting in which he knew his true value.

The lad's revolver flashed. The man nearest to the first machine gun dropped in his track. The second man, Lieutenant Blum, touched the nearest machine gun. Frank's revolver spoke again. The German lieutenant pitched forward on his face.

"So much for you!" cried Frank. He leaped to the bridge and covered the man at the wheel.

"A false move and you are a dead man," he said. "Hold her steady."

A glance told the helmsman that the lad meant what he said. The German kept his hand on the wheel.

Came the cries of men as those released below poured on deck in the wake of Lord Hastings. Frank gazed in that direction. As he did so, the man at the wheel rose suddenly, snatched the revolver from the lad's hand and before Frank could turn, brought it down heavily on his head.

Frank dropped limply to the deck.

The helmsman himself sprang toward the machine gun, while the big vessel, with no hand to guide her wallowed in the trough of the sea.

There came a hoarse command from Lord Hastings, who had seen Frank fall.

Several men fired at the helmsman and he went down. The bridge was unmanned now but its capture was to be no sinecure. The opposition from forward had developed considerable force and the Germans there realized that possession of the bridge by the Americans and Englishmen meant disaster. The third officer, in command, roared out his orders and a score of heavily armed Germans from the forecastle gathered about him.

At Lord Hastings' command, his forces scattered -- it would be every man for himself.

The Germans under the third officer held the forecastle and between them and the opposition amidships was the bridge. Now more men swarmed from aft. The British and Americans were between two fires.

A volley belched from the third officer's men. Two Americans went down. From their scattered positions about the deck, the allies returned the fire, and with effect, as Lord Hastings could see, for several men dropped.

"Good work, men!" shouted Lord Hastings.

The British commander knew that Jack, Tom and the other prisoners would be on deck in a few moments, and that if he could hold the deck until that time, the bridge might be captured by a massed attack.

But now, with the Germans guarding the bridge from the forecastle, it was well nigh impossible, for the allied sailors would be mowed down. For the same reason, the Germens in the forecastle were unable to advance upon the bridge.

Meantime the Vaterland staggered helplessly.

Suddenly there was a wild cry from forward. On deck dashed Jack and the negro, Tom, followed by the released prisoners. The Germans in the forecastle were panic stricken at sight of these unexpected re-enforcements for the opposition. They poured in a withering fire, but it was returned with such deadly effect that the Germans scattered.

But the Germans aft pressed into the heat of the conflict, disregarding shots rained upon them by the allies. Lord Hastings called his men to make a massed stand. They gathered about him and dashed headlong at the Germans.

Revolvers replaced rifles now, for the fighting was at too close quarters for the use of the latter. Men emptied their revolvers in the very faces of their enemies, then clubbed their weapons and continued the struggle.

As the allies turned to meet this attack, the Germans in the forecastle rallied and dashed for the bridge. From behind them, the force led by Jack with Tom flung themselves forward.

At almost the same time consciousness returned to Frank on the bridge. Slowly he raised his head, saw the men approaching him, picked up the revolver that lay near his hand and emptied it into the face of the foe. His second automatic leaped from his pocket and also flashed fire.

Taken by surprise, the Germans hesitated. At the same moment Frank staggered toward the machine guns. He gripped one, whirled it so that it covered the deck.

But he could not fire. Lord Hastings' force was in the line of fire and to have opened up with the rapid-firer would have annihilated the allies as well as the Germans.

A bullet whistled past the lad's head and he ducked instinctively. He emptied the second revolver into the mass of his foes and hurled the now useless weapon in their faces.

Then the Germans were upon him.

But Jack, who realized what would follow should the Germans gain control of the bridge, had urged his men to greater efforts, and these now fell upon the Germans from behind.

With absolute disregard for their own safety, and fighting side by side, Jack and the giant negro forced their way through the struggling mass. The negro wreaked terrible havoc with his deadly pair of brass knuckles, but Jack was giving an equally good account of himself with his two clubbed revolvers.

Two men sprang to the bridge. Frank met the first with a blow of his right fist and the man dropped back. The second made the bridge and Frank grappled with him. The two went down in a heap.

"To the bridge, Tom!" called Jack.

With a desperate effort the two broke through the mass of the enemy and leaped safely to the bridge. Four Germans piled forward with them.

Meantime Lord Hastings' force was so hardly pressed that be for the moment lost sight of the bridge. Under the volleys of the Germans who still stuck to the forecastle, the Americans and English threw themselves to the deck for what little shelter they could find. There they sniped off what numbers of the enemy they could.

Then the Germans who held the forecastle charged.

There was nothing for Lord Hasings to do now but order his men to their feet to meet this situation. At command, they leaped up quickly and presented a solid front to the foe.

In the foremost of the fighting was Captain Stoneman, erstwhile commander of the Algonquin. He had long since discarded his empty automatics to favor of bare fists, and now he flung himself into the midst of the battle. Others sprang forward with him, those who were still armed firing point blank into the mass of the foe.

The Germans gave ground.

The men who had been released last by Jack and the big negro now dashed forward with wild cries of joy and fell upon the enemy from the rear.

On the bridge, Jack, Frank and the negro Tom now were battling with fully a dozen men. No shots were fired. All on the bridge had exhausted their ammunition, and now fell to with butts of revolvers and their naked fists.

"Charge 'em!" shouted Jack suddenly, who realized that the enemy was working back so that they could get their hands on the machine guns.

Frank and the negro asked no questions. Jack dashed forward; they followed him.

"I'm coming, suh!" shouted the negro.

His long arms flew about like flails, and wherever those brass knuckles struck a man went down. Jack felled two men with as many blows. The negro accounted for two more. Frank dropped one to the deck.

There were still seven against three, and the Germans pressed forward with wild cries.

Again the brass knuckles found their mark and a German toppled to the deck. Glancing around, the huge negro saw Frank locked in a close embrace with a powerful German.

The negro stepped back and struck out viciously. The grip on Frank relaxed.

There were but five men to deal with now.

One of these Jack disposed of with a blow to the point of the chin. Frank brought his revolver crashing down on the head of another. Tom's knuckles went home again.

There were only two Germans on the bridge now. These turned to run. Tom stepped forward with quick strides and grasped one by the arm, twisted sharply and sent him hurling into the sea. Then, with the rage of battle still in his heart and before Frank or Jack could stop him, he struck the remaining German a powerful blow in the face. The man crumpled tip and lay still.

The three now were the undisputed masters of the bridge. But along the deck the battle still raged.

Jack sprang to the nearest machine gun. Frank and Tom each manned another.

CHAPTER X
VICTORY

"Never mind that gun, Frank!" shouted Jack. "Take the wheel!"

Frank obeyed without hesitation. He knew that one machine there would be as good as a dozen, and he realized that to keep the big ship on an even keel would be of great assistance.

Again Jack raised his voice. "Lord Hastings!"

His hard pressed commander caught the sound of the lad's voice. He glanced about.

"To the bridge!" cried Jack. "Get out of the line of fire, sir."

Lord Hastings gave a sharp order to his men. Immediately they jumped back, and at a second command, dashed toward the bridge, fully two hundred of them. The others lay about the deck in scattered heaps.

Realizing the import of this ruse, the Germans ran swiftly after them that they too might be out of the line of fire from the machine guns on the bridge.

But the men under Lord Hastings had acted too promptly for the Germans. With the British and Americans out of harm's way, Jack turned the machine gun loose on the deck.

Shrieks and cries arose. Jack stopped his fire.

That single machine gun had done more execution in one single instant than the attacking party had done in the rest of the battle.

"Throw down your arms!" Jack commanded.

The Germans obeyed.

"Jack," said Lord Hastings, "take twenty men and search the ship below. Shoot any man who offers resistance. Tom, take the wheel. Frank, take twenty men and go to the engine room and make prisoners of the stokers."

The two lads hurried away on their several errands.

Frank found the men in the engine room working as though nothing had happened. In some unaccountable manner they had not heard of the fighting above. Frank's men covered them. There was no resistance.

Jack, descending the hatch with his men, encountered opposition in the captain's cabin. Half a dozen men had taken refuge there and refused to emerge.

"Come out or we shall fire through the door!" Jack shouted.

Revolvers spoke from the inside and bullets crashed through the door. This was the German reply.

"Break down the door, men," said Jack quietly.

This was the work of an instant, although one man dropped while it was being done. The door flew inward.

A single volley greeted Jack and his men as they appeared in the doorway but the men had stooped low and none was hit.

Before the Germans could fire again, Jack and his men dashed forward. The Germans were soon overpowered. Jack marched them back on deck.

There Lord Hastings had just accepted the surrender of the vessel from a young ordnance officer, the sole German officer left alive with the exception of Captain Koenig, who was still unconscious in his cabin.

"Jack!" instructed Lord Hastings, "take fifty men and march the prisoners below and lock them up."

Jack touched his cap. "Very good, sir."

He selected his men, surrounded the prisoners and marched them below.

Fank appeared a few moments later with the crew of the engine room. hese, too, were locked up, Lord Hastings detailed some of the victorious seamen for engine room duty, ordered the decks cleared of the dead and injured, and motioned Frank to follow him.

"Mr. Chadwick," he said, "you are my second officer. You will hold the bridge until Mr. Templeton, the first officer, relieves you."

Frank touched his cap and Lord Hastings descended below.

Half an hour later the captured raider got under way. Jack and Lord Hastings were also on the bridge now.

"Shape your course north, sir," said Lord Hastings to Jack.

"North she is, sir," said Jack, passing the word along.

"I suppose you will be interested to know where we are bound?" asked Lord Hastings a few moments later.

"Yes, sir," said Frank and Jack in a single voice.

"New York," said Lord Hastings.

"New York!" echoed Jack. "I supposed of course we were bound for Liverpool or Glasgow."

Lord Hastings smiled.

"No," he said. "I had offered, if successful in this venture, to turn the Vaterland over to the American government. It will be used to transport troops to Europe."

"I see, sir," said Frank. "And when shall we return to England, sir?"

"Not immediately, I believe. We shall probably remain in New York until the first United States expeditionary force sets forth. We shall probably go aboard one of the convoys."

"That suits me, sir," said Jack. "Does it you, Frank?"

"Down to the ground," was Frank's reply.

"Very well," said Lord Hastings. "Mr. Templeton, you will take the bridge. I'll announce the watches later. In the meantime I'll go down and have a talk with my friend, Captain Koenig. Come along, Frank."

Under administering hands Captain Koenig had returned to consciousness. He was in no amiable mood.

"How are you, Captain?" said Lord Hastings cheerfully, as he entered the cabin.

Captain Koenig looked at him with a savage scowl.

"I trust you are feeling better, sir," said Lord Hastings.

"No, I'm not, you blasted Britisher!" said Captain Koenig in very good English.

"I'm sorry, Captain. Is there anything I can do for you until I turn you over to the United States military authorities as a prisoner of war?"

"Not a thing," declared Captain Koenig.

"Too bad," commented Lord Hastings. "What do you say to concluding that game of chess?"

Captain Koenig's reply was a fierce German imprecation.

"Come, Captain," said Lord Hastings, "don't let your temper run away with you. It is very foolish. Why, do you not remember how calmly I took my captivity?"

"You had something up your sleeve," growled Captain Koenig.

"Well, that's true," returned Lord Hastings, "and I'm glad that you haven't. Until we reach New York, Captain, you shall be kept under close guard here. If there is anything you want, please let me know."

Lord Hastings bowed and left the German commander to his own reflections.

Half an hour later, on deck, Frank again encountered Elizabeth Wheaton.

"It was splendid!" exclaimed the girl. "I am so sorry I doubted you in the first place."

"I guess it was only natural," said Frank, with a smile. "I guess I would have done as you did under the circumstances. How is your mother?"

"She is as happy as she can be. She says that she knew the American navy would look out for us."

"You might tell her," said Frank, with a smile, "that it was the British navy that pulled off this job, although I am an American. Lord Hastings and Mr. Templeton are British."

"I guess I won't tell her," laughed the girl. "It would spoil it for her. She thinks there is nothing like the American navy. But what are your duties now?"

"Well," said Frank, "I am the second officer of this ship, rank of lieutenant. Mr. Templeton is the first officer."

"Is that so?" asked the girl in some surprise. "You are so young for such an important position."

Frank turned red.

"I -- I -- I'm not so awfully young," he stammered.

"May be not," admitted Miss Wheaton, with a smile, "but I'll wager you are not over twenty."

"I'm nineteen," said Frank.

"Just a year older than I am," mused the girl, "and still, think of what a lot of excitement you have been through."

"Were you frightened during the fight?" asked Frank, changing the subject.

"Not a bit. I knew you would capture the ship. Mother wasn't frightened either, but some of the others were. It must have been terrible."

"It was," said Frank simply.

Frank took the bridge at 6 o'clock and Jack turned in. And, as the big ship sailed smoothly along during the long hours of the night, Frank gazed out over the deep with a strange sensation in his breast.

He was going back to his own country for the first time in more than three years. He had at this moment one thought in his mind.

"Maybe," he told himself over and over through the night, "maybe I shall have time to go home and see father!"

CHAPTER XI
NEW YORK

News of the capture of the German raider Vaterland had preceded the vessel into New York, having been flashed by wireless while the ship was still several days out. Therefore there was a large crowd on hand to see the Vaterland anchor in the North River. Lord Hastings surrendered the vessel to American naval authorities and then the officers, crew, erstwhile prisoners and German captives all went ashore.

Captain Koenig and his crew were taken in charge by the authorities and a few days later were sent to one of the big American internment camps in the south, where they would remain until the end of the war.

There was considerable cheering as Lord Hastings and his officers stepped ashore. The British commander dodged as much of this as possible and with Jack and Frank jumped into a taxicab and were driven to the Biltmore, where they registered and were assigned to a suite of rooms. There, Lord Hastings decided, they would remain pending instructions.

The successful capture of the Vaterland was flashed across the Atlantic to the British admiralty and a cable message of congratulations was received a short time later, together with orders for Lord Hastings to remain in New York until other orders reached him.

It was at the dinner table that evening that Frank asked Lord Hastings' permission to run home for a day or two. Lord Hastings assented readily, for he knew that Frank naturally was anxious to see his father.

"Why don't you take Jack with you?" he asked.

"I shall be glad to," replied Frank. "Do you want to go, Jack?"

"Sure," said the young Englishman. "I shall be glad."

"How about you, Lord Hastings?" questioned Frank. "I should like to have you go also."

"I appreciate your invitation," said Lord Hastings, with a smile, "but I thought I would run over to Washington and see the British ambassador. But you see if you can't bring your father back to New York with you, Frank. I should be more than pleased to see him."

"I'll see what I can do, sir," replied the lad.

Thus it was arranged. Jack and Frank took a train for Boston early the following morning and Lord Hastings caught a train for Washington.

"You should have sent your father a telegram, Frank," said Jack, as they left the train in Boston.

"I want to take him by surprise."

"Maybe he won't be home."

"By George! I hadn't thought of that. I guess he will be, though. He's usually home in the afternoon."

The boys took the elevated from the South station to the North station, where they found they could catch a train to Woburn, the town where Frank's father lived, in ten minutes.

It was only a little more than ten miles from Boston to Woburn and the trip was made quickly. As they alighted from the train, Frank let his eyes rove over the familiar landmarks, which he had not seen for three years. There was little change to be noticed. Frank led the way toward his home.

He paused before an old-fashioned New England house and Jack, glancing up, saw this sign on the door:

"Dr. R. G. Chadwick."

Frank mounted the steps rapidly and rang the bell. An elderly woman came to the door. Frank had never seen her before.

"Is the doctor in?" he asked.

"Yes, but he is busy right now. Step in and have a seat."

Frank led the way into the doctor's waiting room, where he and Jack sat down.

Frank's mother was dead. She had passed away when the lad was not more than five years, and in the days that followed Dr. Chadwick had been father and mother both to him.

From the little room beyond Frank caught the sound of his father's voice. The lad could hardly, restrain his impatience.

A few moments later, however, a door slammed, signifying that the physician's patient had left by, another door. A moment more and the door into the waiting room was flung open and Dr. Chadwick stepped into the room.

He looked at the two figures who now rose to greet him, and then he jumped forward with a cry.

"Frank!"

A moment and the lad was in his father's arms.

Dr. Chadwick held the lad off at arm's length and looked at him.

"You've grown," he said. "Sit down and tell me about yourself. I was afraid you had been killed. I haven't had a letter from you for almost a year."

"Before I recount my adventures, father," said Frank, "I want you to meet my chum, Jack Templeton, of whom I have written you."

Jack and Dr. Chadwick shook hands. Then Frank sat down and gave an account of his adventures in the three years since he had been separated from his father in Naples, Italy, soon after the great European war had broken out.

"And you say your commander, Lord Hastings, is in New York?" said his father.

"He's in Washington today, sir," said Jack, "but he probably will be back day after tomorrow, when we must return, sir."

"I shall do myself the honor of calling on him," declared Dr. Chadwick.

"He asked me particularly to bring you back with us, father," said Frank. "I'm glad you will go."

"Of course I'll go," said Dr. Chadwick. "Now, son, I have a patient to see, so if you and Jack care to you can go down the street. You may see some of your old friends."

Jack and Frank were the heroes of the town the two days they remained in Woburn. Frank saw many of his old friends, and there is many a lad in the American navy today who enlisted as a result of Frank's harrangue that he answer his country's call.

True to his word, Dr. Chadwick accompanied the lads back to New York. Lord Hastings had returned to the metropolis ahead of them, and was in their room when they arrived. The boys' commander and Frank's father shook hands warmly, and the lads withdrew to let them talk.

Over the dinner table that evening Lord Hastings recounted some of Frank's adventures which the lad had been too modest to tell. Dr. Chadwick listened eagerly.

"It is as I would have had him do," he exclaimed.

"When I lost him in Naples I was terribly worried and I had the police scour the city for him. At last I gave up hope that he was still alive and returned home. Then I received a letter from Frank telling me that he had joined the British navy.

"I am of old English descent and naturally enough my sympathies were always with the Allies. Therefore I sanctioned Frank's choice, but I have been fearful that I would never see him again."

"How long will you stay in New York, Lord Hastings?"

"It's too bad," said Lord Hastings, "but we shall leave here in the morning."

"Is that so, sir?" exclaimed Frank eagerly.

"Where to, sir?"

"We have been ordered to Halifax," was Lord Hastings' reply. "There I shall take command of the British cruiser Lawrence. We will be one of the convoy to protect the crossing of the first contingent of American troops."

"I am sorry it is so soon," said Dr. Chadwick. "However, what must be, must be."

In spite of the fact that Frank hated to leave his father so soon again, he nevertheless was glad that the time of inaction was comparatively short. Jack also showed his pleasure at Lord Hastings' announcement.

Dr. Chadwick remained i New York over night as the guest of Lord Hastings. The four had breakfast together and then all repaired to the North station, where Dr. Chadwick took a train for Woburn and Lord Hastings and his two officers boarded a through train for Canada.

"How does it happen," asked Frank, as they rode along that afternoon, "that American troops will go across by the way of Halifax?"

"Submarines," returned Lord Hastings. "The channel from Halifax is well guarded, and it is believed that there is less danger by traversing that route."

"Have you any idea how many men will form the first contingent?" asked Frank.

"No, I haven't," replied Lord Hastings. "That is something that is being well guarded by the United States war department. It is just as well, too. Nevertheless, I understand that there will be several large transports, at least."

The trio reached the Canadian city the following day, and Lord Hastings at once reported himself to the British commandant. Before evening Lord Hastings had taken command of the Lawrence. As of yore, Jack and Frank were his first and second officers.

"And when will we sail, sir?" asked Jack.

"Tomorrow at nightfall," was his commander's reply.

Jack and Frank turned in early. They were happy and eager for action.

CHAPTER XII
ACROSS THE ATLANTIC

The first contingent of American troops to cross the Atlantic to take their places on the firing line sailed in three divisions. Approximately 225,000 troops comprised the contingent.

The transports, on their voyage, were convoyed by British and American torpedo boats destroyers, cruisers and other ships of war. These were in sufficient number, American and British naval authorities believed, to protect the transports should they be attacked by German submarines.

The transports themselves carried big guns fore and aft and were so equipped as to be able to give a good account of themselves should occasion arise; and as the voyage progressed a sharp lookout was kept aboard every vessel of the flotilla, that a submarine might not come unheralded within striking distance of the transports or their convoy.

Much to the disappointment of Jack and Frank,

they did not sail with the first section of the American troops; nor did they find themselves with the second. In fact, it seemed to both lads that they were to be denied the honor of the trip altogether. But in this belief they were wrong.

The British cruiser Lawrence, under command of Lord Hastings, with Jack as first officer and Frank the third in command, was ordered forth from a Canadian port as one of the convoy for the third section.

American troops were being transported to France by this northern route because naval authorities believed the route was less likely to be infested with German submarines. The channel was well defined and well protected. Thus, the American navy department had little fear that the troops would be landed safely.

It was a clear morning in May that the flotilla put to sea. The sailing was without ostentation, though the population of the port was aware that the start was being made. However, the sailing was kept secret from the rest of the world -- even from the United States, except the naval authorities -- for the navy department was doing everything possible to prevent word of the sailing from reaching the enemy.

But for this fact it is highly probable that the first contingent of American troops would not have reached France safely, or at least with more danger than attended their crossing, for the United States at that time was infested with German spies, who, through secret channels -- via Argentina and Sweden, as it developed later -- were able to flash their discoveries to the Imperial German government in Berlin.

There was no demonstration, then -- such as had attended sailing of similar expeditions when Uncle Sam went to war -- in the Canadian city the troops had just left. The city went about its business as though nothing out of the ordinary was going on.

The last of the troops had been ordered aboard the transports the night before and assigned to quarters. Therefore, some of the men were still asleep in their bunks when the flotilla lifted anchor and put to sea.

There were five transports filled with American soldiers. Three cruisers and a pair of torpedo boat destroyers showed the way. Strung out on either side of the transports, which proceeded singly one behind the other, were two cruisers and as many of the smaller craft. A pair of American cruisers brought up the rear. Altogether, it was a formidable armada that steamed swiftly across the Atlantic.

The Lawrence, aboard which Jack and Frank served as officers, had been assigned a post of honor in the first line. To port was the destroyer Halifax. To starboard was nothing but the expanse of the ocean. The Lawrence was on the end of the first line.

The first day passed quietly. The ships of war were all stripped for action and the men stood to their posts during the long day. There was little probability that a German submarine lurked so close to North American shores, but the American and British commanders were taking no chances.

Frank, appearing to relieve Jack on the bridge at eight bells that evening, smiled.

"Guess there will be no excitement on this voyage," he said to his friend.

Jack shrugged his shoulders.

"Hard to tell," he replied. "However, I don't anticipate any trouble until we are near the coast of Ireland."

He went below without further words and turned in.

The second day passed quietly, and the third. Noon of the fourth day out, however, saw the allied American and British convoy in action.

Jack held the bridge at the time. Frank and Lord Hastings were below in the latter's cabin. Jack was gazing straight ahead.

Suddenly there was a crash-crash of heavy, guns as the starboard turret forward aboard the Lawrence poured forth a salvo. Jack wheeled about suddenly. Across the sea he made out what he felt sure was a periscope of a German submarine.

At the same moment the forward starboard battery belched forth again. The gunners had not waited for the word to fire. Such had been their instructions when the voyage began, and they were still effective.

Jack took command now, pending the arrival of Lord Hastings from his cabin below. At the same moment a second and a third periscope, still some distance away, came into view.

"Aft, there!" cried Jack, and the batteries in the stern opened upon the submarines.

Jack signaled the engine room for full speed ahead and at a word to the helmsman the Lawrence swung sharply and headed for the nest of submarines.

Lord Hastings appeared on deck at this moment, closely followed by Frank. The commander of the Lawrence took in the situation at a glance.

"Wireless the two cruisers to keep position," he shouted to Frank. "Order the destroyers to follow us. There may be more of the enemy to port," he explained.

Frank passed the word and the fourth officer dashed for the wireless room.

A moment later the two cruisers to port, which had swerved with the apparent intention of following the Lawrence toward the foe, swung back into position, as did the vessels that guarded the transports on the port side. The two destroyers, however, veered sharply and dashed after the Lawrence.

Again, at Lord Hastings' command, the three cruisers protecting the transports to starboard also remained in line. This, Lord Hastings explained later, he had deemed advisable because a submarine might have pushed a torpedo through to a transport had they moved out of line.

One of the cruisers making up the rear guard, however, the American cruiser Huron, dashed toward the submarines.

And now it became apparent that there were not only three submarines to contend, with - there were at least five or six. The flotilla had run into a veritable nest of the undersea terrors.

The submarines now rose to the surface and launched torpedoes. The distance was still great, however, and none of them found its mark.

In the meantime the guns aboard the two cruisers rumbled as they bore down on the foe, and the destroyers, not far behind, added their voices to the conflict.

Lord Hastings, as he took command of the situation, realized that Jack had acted with promptness upon the discovery of the foe and he commended the lad with a nod of his head.

Suddenly there came a cry of triumph from the forward turret aboard the Lawrence. A British shell had struck squarely aboard the nearest submersible. The little vessel seemed to fly into a thousand pieces. A moment later it disappeared from sight.

A second mighty cheer rang out.

"It's not all over yet," said Jack grimly.

Frank, who overheard the words, nodded his assent.

At a quick command from Lord Hastings the Lawrence veered sharply to starboard -- and a torpedo from the nearest submarine flashed by harmlessly.

"Pretty close, though," Frank muttered.

It had been close, and had it not been for the prompt action of Lord Hastings in maneuvering the vessel out of harm's way, the Lawrence would have received a death blow.

Before the submarine could launch a second torpedo, a shell from the Huron struck her squarely amidships. A moment later the second submarine disappeared beneath the water.

Again a combined British and American cheer rang out over the sea.

So far as those aboard the Lawrence could see now, there were still four of the submarines in action. This was a formidable number indeed, and Lord Hastings realized that it would take quick and decisive action if they were to be disposed of before severe injury could be inflicted upon the British and American ships.

He turned to Frank. "Order the Sandusky to our assistance!" he commanded.

Frank dashed to the wireless room. A few moments later the Sandusky, an American cruiser, which was one of the rear guard, left her place in the line and dashed forward.

"Now we'll get 'em!" cried Frank.

CHAPTER XIII
END OF THE SUBMARINE FLEET

There were now opposed to the four remaining submarines, two American and one British cruiser and two British torpedo destroyers. Two U-boats had been sunk by the allied fleet and so far the submarines had failed to deliver an effective blow.

Lord Hastings now commanded his ships to spread out a trifle more -- this giving them more room to act while at the same time interposing an effective barrier against torpedoes before the transports.

Aboard these transports the men were straining their eyes to get a view of the battle and chafing at their inability to take a hand. And yet there was hardly a man aboard the transports who did not realize that in an encounter with a submarine, a troop ship nine times out of ten would come off second best.

Denied the privilege of taking a hand, therefore, they stood at the rails of the various ships and cheered on the fighting vessels.

There was an explosion as a torpedo found the hull of the destroyer Halifax. The ship wabbled crazily in her course, then dashed forward again. Apparently she was not badly hurt.

A shell from one of the guns mounted by the first submarine, a moment later, landed squarely aboard the same destroyer and carried away her superstructure. Men fell to the deck dead or badly wounded.

"First blood for the Germans," said Jack to himself.

Apparently angered at this German success, the second British destroyer, the Angelic, darted forward and attacked the submarine with such abandon and effectiveness that she was forced to give the destroyer its entire attention. Twice the Angelic maneuvered out of the path of a torpedo, and then, with a well directed shot, put the submarine out of the battle. This shell caught the U-boat along side the conning tower. Iron and steel flew high in the air, and, descending, scattered death among the crew. Thus crippled, a second shot from the Angelic disposed of her entirely and she sank beneath the waves.

There were now but three submarines left.

"Great Scott! It's a wonder they don't submerge," said Frank. "Wonder if they think they can lick us?"

The answer came from the enemy. All three simultaneously launched torpedoes at the Lawrence. It was absolutely impossible for Lord Hastings to maneuver the ship out of the way of all three missiles. He did the best he could, but one of the projectiles penetrated the side of the ship and pierce the engine room.

There was a loud explosion from below. Lord Hastings turned to Frank.

"Go below and report," he said quietly.

Frank hurried away. Meanwhile, unmindful that the Lawrence might have received a vital wound, Lord Hastings pressed even closer toward the enemy.

In the boiler room Frank found confusion. Three men had been killed by the explosion. Half a dozen others had been wounded by pieces of flying steel or splinters, while several had been badly scalded by escaping water and steam.

Frank approached McMullen, the chief engineer.

"What's your damage?" he asked.

"Just what you see," replied the engineer, with a wave of his band.

"We're still able to proceed?"

"Yes, sir; and we are proceeding."

Frank could see that this was right. He went on deck again.

"Three killed and a dozen wounded, sir," he reported to Lord Hastings. "No vital damage, sir."

"Very good!" returned Lord Hastings, and turned away with a command for Jack.

The British vessels were now pouring such a stream of shells upon the enemy that it seemed impossible the submarines could survive. But the little craft stuck doggedly to their work and launched torpedo after torpedo at the British and Americans.

"Looks like they had decided to lick us or to go down fighting," Frank said to Jack.

"If that's the case," was Jack's reply, "they'll go down fighting."

The German submarines made no offer to retreat. They stood their ground bravely enough.

Suddenly one of them blew up with a loud explosion. A shot from the cruiser Sandusky had found its mark.

"Only two now," said Frank. "Surely they, won't continue the fight."

But continue the fight the Germans did. Another torpedo struck the Lawrence forward and exploded with a loud detonation. The Lawrence staggered a trifle, but moved forward. Apparently the wound was not serious.

The British and Americans were right upon them now. Regardless of possible torpedoes, Lord Hastings pressed on. He knew that he now had the two remaining submarines in his grasp, and that while it was possible a torpedo would dispose of the Lawrence, other British and American ships would account for the enemy. Therefore, while not exposing himself needlessly, he advanced with more abandon than before.

One, two torpedoes exploded forward and each time the Lawrence staggered. Then the moment for which Lord Hastings had been waiting presented itself.

A brief command to the helmsman and the Lawrence again veered sharply. She headed straight for the nearest submarine, now only yards away. In vain the German commander attempted to get his boat out of harm's way. The sharp prow of the Lawrence found its mark and the German submarine was crushed like an egg shell.

So there was but one of the enemy left afloat.

"We'll lose him, sure," said Jack, alarmed that - one of the enemy might escape. "He'll submerge."

Indeed, it seemed that this would have been the wise thing to do. Instead, however, a white flag appeared from the periscope.

"Great Scott! Surrender!" cried Frank. "I wonder why? All he had to do was submerge."

Jack shrugged his shoulders.

"Too deep for me," he said. "However, I guess the German commander has had fighting a-plenty."

At the appearance of the white flag the British ships ceased their fire. A German appeared through the conning tower. He carried signal flags, which he waved. The signal officer aboard the Lawrence replied.

"Says he has surrendered and that he and his men will come aboard, sir," reported the signal officer.

"I read him," returned Lord Hastings, to whom signaling was no secret. "Tell him we'll send boats for him and his men and to be ready, for we shall sink his vessel as soon as all are safely aboard the Lawrence."

Again the flags flashed their message. Then the German disappeared. He came on deck again a moment later, however. Men followed him. Lord Hastings ordered several small boats launched, and these put off toward the submarine.

"You can't tell me," said Frank to Jack, "that everything is right. There is something funny about this."

"Well, what is it?" demanded Jack.

"I don't know what it is, but I've a feeling --"

Frank broke off suddenly and ran to Lord Hastings.

"Treachery!" he cried. "There is something wrong, sir."

Lord Hastings looked at the lad in amazement.

"What's that?" he demanded.

"There is something wrong, sir," said Frank quickly. "I have a feeling that the Germans are plotting treachery."

Lord Hastings smiled.

"I guess it's too late for that," he said grimly.

"However, I'm glad you warned me. I'll take the necessary precaution. Have one of the forward guns trained on the submarine, Mr. Chadwick."

Frank hurried away with a feeling of some relief, but he was not fully satisfied.

The gun trained on the submarine, he stood by quietly.

Apparently all the Germans were now on the deck of the little submarine. The British small boats had approached close -- almost close enough to take off the German crew and the German commander.

Suddenly there was a hiss from the submarine. A torpedo flashed from the side of the little vessel. It whizzed past the Lawrence and sped straight toward the closest American transport.

Frank gave a cry of alarm and then commanded the man who stood by the gun already trained on the submarine: "Fire!"

"Boom!" the big gun spoke.

Then there came a terrific explosion. The German submarine, with its officers and crew upon its deck, was hurled high in the air as the Lawrence's shell burst squarely amidships. It came down in a million pieces.

Alongside, the British boats sent to take off the Germans rocked crazily for several moments on the angry waves. When these became still, there was no German nor submarine to be seen.

Thanks to the watchfulness of the commander of the transport, the ship had been able to escape the torpedo so treacherously launched by the Germans; so no harm had been done.

Lord Hastings approached Frank and laid a hand on his shoulder.

"Quick work, Frank," he said. "I should have listened to you. However, nothing has come of the treachery. But I have learned that there is nothing sacred in the

Hun mind. I shall never trust another German!"

CHAPTER XIV
UNDER OLD GLORY

The third section of the first contingent of American troops sent to France reached the shores of England safely. After several days of parading and celebrating they were transported to France and soon they reached the field of battle, where, for the next few months, they would undergo the intensive training that would fit them to take up their share of the work along with their British and French allies.

When the transports docked safely in a British port the duties of Frank and Jack ceased so far as they had to do with the American troops. Lord Hastings turned the command of the Lawrence over to a brother officer and with Frank and Jack took train for London. The lads accompanied Lord Hastings; to his home, where they awaited further instructions.

These instructions came sooner than they had dared hope.

It was at dinner the second day after their return that a peculiar smile on Lord Hastings' face told Jack and Frank that there was something in the air.

Jack restrained his impatience; not so Frank.

"I have a hunch that something is going to happen," he said over the dessert.

"That so?" queried Lord Hastings. "Just what, for instance?"

"Well, I don't know exactly, sir," was the lad's reply, "but it wouldn't surprise me greatly if Jack and I were soon on active service."

"And what makes you think so?" asked Lord Hastings.

"You do, sir. I can tell from your expression that you have good news for us."

"Then I must learn to control my face better," said Lord Hastings. "However, Frank, seeing that you are so impatient, I may as well admit it right now."

"I knew it!" exclaimed Frank joyfully. "What is it, sir?"

"If you will just hold your horses a bit, I'll tell you," was his commander's reply. "It seems to me that you promised to restrain your impatience."

"So I did, sir," replied Frank, flushing a trifle. "I will try to remember that promise."

"Do," replied Lord Hastings, and continued:

"I don't know just how you'll like this piece I of work, but some one has to do it and I volunteered your services."

"We are always glad to help in any way possible, sir," said Jack quietly. Lord Hastings nodded.

"That's why I took the liberty of offering your services without first having consulted you," he made reply. "Well, then, tomorrow morning you will report to Captain Glenn aboard the Albatross."

"The American ship Albatross!" exclaimed Frank. "That's a merchant ship, sir."

"So it is," agreed his commander. "It is now an armed merchant ship, to be more precise, it plies between Liverpool and Halifax. Its main cargo from this time forth will be food and other supplies for the American expeditionary forces. You will report to Captain Glenn as his first and second officers. As a result of the United States' declaration of war on Germany there is a dearth of young officers. Most of them have joined the naval forces of the nation. In reality, Captain Glenn is an American naval officer, and now that the United States has declared war, the Albatross may be classed as an American naval vessel. It has been heavily armed that it may make the voyages without convoy. There will be considerable danger, of course, but I know you are not the lads to shirk that. Come, now, what do you say?"

"We accept, of course, sir," said Frank. "But are you not going with us?"

"No," said Lord Hastings, "I have other work to do here. But I hope to be able to make use of your services before many days."

"I am sorry you are not going, sir," said Jack, "but I guess that can't be helped. We shall report to Captain Glenn in the morning. I take that to mean that we must leave London tonight?"

"Exactly," was Lord Hastings' reply. "I believe Captain Glenn has arranged to sail by 8 o'clock."

"Then we may as well pack up, Frank," said Jack.

The two lads made their way to their rooms and got together what belongings they considered necessary. Lord Hastings accompanied them to the station, where they took train for Liverpool.

"You will find Captain Glenn a very agreeable commander, I am sure," said Lord Hastings. "Good-bye and good luck, boys."

The lads shook hands with Lord Hastings and he was gone.

Arriving in Liverpool late that evening they put up at a hotel for the night and early the following morning sought out the Albatross and went aboard.

At the rail a young man -- he could not have been more than 30 -- watched them calmly as they came over the side. He was attired in a pair of dark blue trousers and a blue coat. He wore no insignia of rank. There was no other person in sight. The two lads approached him.

"Can you tell us where we will find Captain Glenn?" asked Jack.

"I'm Captain' Glenn," was the other's response. Jack was a little surprised, for he had naturally surmised Captain Glenn would be an older man. The latter noticed Jack's confusion and smiled.

"You're Lieutenant Templeton, I suppose?" he questioned.

"Yes, sir," replied Jack.

"Good!" The captain extended a hand which Jack grasped. Captain Glenn turned to Frank.

"Lieutenant Chadwick?" he questioned.

"Yes, sir," returned Frank, and grasped the captain's hand.

"Very good," said Captain Glenn. "Mr. Templeton, you are the first officer of this ship and Mr. Chadwick, you are next in command. Come below to my cabin and I will give you our course and other details."

The lads followed him below. The captain explained things in a few words and after showing them to their quarters he added:

"We sail at 8 o'clock. It is now 7."

Jack and Frank ascended the bridge fifteen minutes later. Signs of life became apparent aboard the Albatross. Both lads assumed their duties at once and soon the Albatross was moving out to sea.

The Albatross, the lads learned, was one of the largest freighters afloat. It carried a crew of more than 200 men. It was loaded in ballast for the trip across, but, returning, it would carry a valuable cargo of food and supplies.

The third officer's name was Williams. He was a Welshman. Others of importance aboard were Carney, chief engineer; Tompkins, bo's'n; Washington, negro cook and Paul, wireless operator.

Jack was assigned to the first watch. Frank came next in line and then Williams. Captain Glenn announced that he himself would take the bridge whenever necessary.

Soon after the Albatross had sailed members of the crew were picked for the various watches, Captain Glenn retained the bridge until the ship was well out to sea.

Frank and Jack saw that the Albatross was heavily armed for a trade ship. Forward she was equipped with a battery of 6-inch guns, while a second battery had been constructed aft. She also carried two 6-inch torpedoes.

"We should be able to give a good account of ourselves," said Frank, after a survey of the vessel.

"Rather," said Jack dryly; "and remember, we are to have the guns ready for action every instant."

"I'm not likely to forget," said Frank; "and don't you forget that orders are to keep the searchlight playing at night."

"I won't be any more likely to forget than you are," said Jack, with a smile. "Remember, we're not out hunting for Germans now. We're trying to dodge them."

"I know it," said Frank. "That's the trouble with a merchant ship. We'll run while we can and then fight instead of fighting first and running if we have to."

"Can't be helped now," said Jack. "We're here and we shall have to make the best of it."

"Well, you can't tell," replied Frank. "Something is likely to turn up any time."

"Right; but we're here to see that it doesn't turn up if we can help it. Well, I'm going below. Call me if you want anything."

"Don't worry," said Frank with a smile. "I guess nothing is going to happen, but if it does you may make sure that you'll hear about it."

Jack went below and turned in for a good night's sleep. Frank held the bridge.

Nothing happened that night nor the following day or night, but when Captain Glenn came on deck the morning of the third day he cast an uneasy eye toward the northeast.

"Storm brewing," he said quietly to Frank, who stood near.

"Calm enough now, sir," returned Frank. "Sun shinning, too, sir. Doesn't look as though there would be much of a blow."

"What's the barometer say?" asked Captain Glenn.

Frank took a hasty look. "Falling, sir."

"As I thought. We're in for a spell of bad weather. Pipe all hands on deck, Mr. Chadwick."

Frank gave the necessary command. As the first man appeared from below, the sun went out as if a great cloud had blotted it from sight. Outside it became black as right.

CHAPTER XV
THE STORM

Despite his lack of years, Captain Glenn was an able skipper; otherwise he would not have been in command of the Albatross. He acted promptly and with decision.

Men dashed forward and aft as Frank and Jack repeated the captain's commands. Everything was made secure before the storm broke and Captain Glenn ordered all men not needed on deck below. The helmsman had lashed himself to the wheel. Everything was as snug as it could be made aboard the Albatross.

Captain Glenn signaled the engine room for five knots.

"We'll have to slow down," he explained to Jack.

"No need of rushing blindly into the storm. It's coming from the northeast. We'll hold to our course as well as possible. The Albatross has weathered many a hard gale. Guess we will come through this all right."

The words had hardly left his mouth when the gale descended with the utmost fury. The Albatross keeled to port until her side almost touched the water. Jack, Frank and the captain saved themselves from being washed overboard by seizing the rail and clutching it with all their strength. As the ship righted itself, only to keel far to starboard the next minute, a deluge of water covered the deck.

Captain Glenn bellowed a hoarse command to Jack and Frank.

"Below and get into your oilskins!" he shouted.

The two lads struggled along the deck holding fast to whatever they could find. The ship rocked and dipped like a drunken man. Frank and Jack clambered into their oilskins with difficulty and then made their way back to the bridge, where Captain Glenn stood drenched to the skin.

The latter turned the bridge over to Jack while he went below for dry clothes and his own oilskins.

"Keep her on her course!" he shouted. "We're in no danger."

Jack obeyed. Captain Glenn returned a short time later and again assumed command.

All that day the gale raged and with the coming of night it showed no signs of abatement. So far the Albatross had plowed through the turbulent sea without injury, but it was plain to Jack and Frank that Captain Glenn was growing uneasy.

"This gale must stop soon or we'll have trouble," he shouted. "A ship can stand only so much pounding and you can hear the Albatross straining now."

It was true. Even above the roar of the gale the lads could hear the creaking of the timbers as the Albatross fought her way through the raging sea.

A man appeared from below.

"Sprung a leak forward, sir!" he shouted.

"Mr. Chadwick!" commanded Captain Glenn. "Get below and find out from the carpenter how bad the leak is."

Frank returned fifteen minutes later.

"Not bad, sir," he reported. "Carpenter says he can fix it in two hours. Could do it in half an hour if it weren't for the storm."

Captain Glenn nodded but made no audible reply.

At midnight the gale was still raging. Captain Glenn, tired out, announced that he was going below to get "forty winks." Jack took the bridge.

"Call me if anything happens," were the commander's last words as he went below.

Along toward four o'clock a man emerged from below and fought his way toward the bridge.

"Leak in the main compartment aft, sir," he reported to Jack.

Jack ordered Frank below to learn the extent of the damage.

"Pretty bad this time, Jack," said Frank, reporting a few minutes later. "We're shipping water by the gallon. Carpenter says he can't do a thing. However, one compartment more or less won't hurt. She'll still float."

"All right," Jack replied. "I won't awake Captain Glenn until I have to."

An hour later Captain Glenn, greatly refreshed, reappeared on deck. Jack reported the damage. Captain Glenn accepted the bad news with a nod, summoned Williams, the fourth officer, and ordered Jack and Frank below.

"Get some sleep," he shouted to make himself heard above the roaring of the wind. "I'll call you if you're needed."

The two lads descended to their quarters. It had been many hours since they had slept and in spite of the rolling and pitching of the ship they were asleep the moment they touched their bunks.

And as they slept the gale raged.

On the evening of the second night, with the gale still at its height, Captain Glenn said, "Six more hours of this and we are done for."

At that time the Albatross was leaking badly in a dozen places. The engineer was having trouble with his engines. The rolling and pitching of the ship made it almost impossible to stand.

Suddenly the ship gave a great lurch, keeled over, righted, and then wallowed in the trough of the sea.

"Great Scott!" ejaculated Frank. "Now what?"

"Rudder broken, sir," said the helmsman quietly.

Frank threw up his hands in a gesture of dismay. "That settles it," he declared.

"Out with the life boats!" cried Captain Glenn.

"All hands on deck."

The men needed no urging. The life boats were made ready, the men the while clinging to whatever support offered itself. Suddenly there was a shrill scream aft, followed by a cry: "Man overboard!"

Captain Glenn shrugged his shoulders.

"Can't be helped," he said. "He's just beating us a little; that's all."

The commander of the Albatross hesitated to give the command to lower the boats. He knew that the odds were a hundred to one that the boats would not live in such a sea. While the Albatross held together they were safer aboard the vessel.

Came a wave sweeping over the ship mightier than the rest. The Albatross dipped clear to the sea. For a moment it seemed that she must go under; but she righted herself with an effort.

"Thought we were gone for that time!" shouted Captain Glenn. "She won't survive another. Lower away the boats, men."

Half a dozen men had been washed overboard by the last mighty deluge; the others now sprang to the boats and lowered them. Several were swamped as they hit the water, and there were not more than half a dozen that put off from the ship.

In the last boat were Frank, Jack and Captain Glenn and the fourth officer, Williams.

The little boat hit the water with a splash and all but turned over.

"Shove away from the ship!" cried Captain Glenn to the two sailors who manned the boat -- the others had been lost. The sailors, Timothy and Allen by names, obeyed and then all took to their oars.

The little boat, one moment riding the crest of the waves, the next wallowing in the trough of the sea, moved away bravely though every moment it seemed in imminent danger of capsizing. It took skillful handling by Captain Glenn -- the only man not at the oars -- to keep the craft right side up.

It was so dark there on the sea that it was impossible for the occupants of the boat to tell whether or not others had escaped the ship safely.

"This storm can't last much longer, sir!" shouted Jack.

"If it does, we are wasting energy rowing," said Frank quietly.

"We'll row along as long as we can," said Captain Glenn. "We've been blown so far off our course that there is no telling where we are. It wouldn't surprise me if we had been blown off the coast of South America."

"Impossible, sir," ejaculated Jack.

"Maybe so," replied Captain Glenn. "I'm just guessing. Still, it wouldn't surprise me a bit."

Suddenly the raging wind ceased. The waves still rose to mighty heights, but the wind was stilled almost to a zephyr and the little boat rode the swells gently.

"It's over, sir!" shouted Frank.

"So it is," said Captain Glenn, "but it is still dark. Strike a match someone and learn the hour."

Jack did so.

"Three thirty, sir," he said.

"Morning or afternoon?" demanded Frank, who seemed to have lost track of the time entirely.

"Morning, of course," said Jack.

"Can't see the reason for that 'of course,'" mumbled Frank.

"It should be light in half an hour," said Captain Glenn. "Then we may see whether any of the others are near."

They waited silently. The sea grew calmer and calmer; and at last the light came.

The occupants of the boat stood up and scanned the ocean. There was nothing that the eye could see save water. There was no sign of the Albatross nor other of the small boats.

"Poor fellows!" said Jack.

At that moment Frank, his eyes sharper than those of the others, gave an exclamation. "Land ahead!" he shouted.

CHAPTER XVI
ASHORE

It was still early morning when the little boat with the six castaways -- Frank, Jack, Captain Glenn, Williams, fourth officer of the Albatross' and the two sailors, Timothy and Allen -- rounded a projecting point of land and put into a small harbor.

Along the shore were signs of human hands. There was a recently constructed dock, well hidden under overhanging foliage. It was perfectly invisible from a distance, being revealed to view only when the small boat approached within a hundred yards. There was no vessel in sight.

"Somebody lives around these parts, that's sure," commented Captain Glenn. "Wonder where we are, anyhow?"

"Thought you said something about South America, Sir," said Frank.

"So I did," replied the erstwhile commander of the Albatross, "but that's no reason we are. I was just guessing at it, you know."

"Well," said Jack, "we're safe at any rate, and that's something."

"Right you are, Jack," said Frank. "I am sorry the same cannot be said for all who were with us aboard the Albatross."

For a time the occupants of the boat were silent as they drew closer to the shore. At last the nose of the little craft plowed into the sand. Frank leaped lightly ashore and the others followed.

"Drag the boat out of the water, Allen," Frank instructed, and added: "We don't want it to be carried away by the tide."

The sailor followed instructions and the little boat was soon high and dry.

"Now what?" asked Jack.

"Well," said Captain Glenn, "I don't know where we are exactly and the best thing is to find out. I still incline to the belief that we're on the coast of South America and the more I look around the more certain I feet about it. It has all the appearance of the tropics."

"We'll have a look, then, sir," said Frank briefly.

"Hold on," called Jack, as Frank moved away. "Don't forget we've rifles in the boat."

"Guess we won't need them," said Frank. "We're out of the war zone, at least."

"Don't be so sure, youngster," interposed Williams, himself a man well over forty. "This war has pretty well dragged every nation beneath the sun within its maw. You never can tell where you will encounter the hand of the German Kaiser; and, besides, we'll need something to eat."

"Right, Williams," said Captain Glenn, "and wherever you find the Kaiser's band there you also will find trouble. The German is no respecter of neutrality, or anything else, for that matter. We'll take our rifles and make sure that our revolvers and knives are in working order."

The six returned to the boat, from which Frank dragged a dozen rifles and a quantity of superfluous revolvers and sheath knives.

There's an abundance here," the lad said. "We can carry two revolvers apiece and a knife. Also we can lug a rifle, but I am opposed to carrying more than one."

"I'm with you there," said Captain Glenn. "For that reason I shall detail you, Chadwick, to guard the boat with Timothy and Allen, while Templeton, Williams and I do a little exploring."

Frank's face fell a trifle, for he was keen to have a hand in the work; but he was too well trained to protest. So all he said was: "Very well, sir."

"In the meantime," continued Captain Glenn, is you might drag out all the ammunition and provisions and make sure that they're dry. It will be well to provide against eventualities. Should we fail to return by 4 o'clock this afternoon, you will know that something has gone wrong and you will look to your own safety without thought of help from us."

"Very well, sir," said Frank again.

Captain Glenn now led the way inland, Jack and Williams striding along on either side of him. Each carried a rifle in addition to a pair of Colt automatics and a heavy sheath knife stuck in his belt. They felt perfectly able to cope with any danger that might present itself.

Behind, Frank and the two sailors fell to unloading the boat. It had been well stocked with provision, water and ammunition. Such a contingency as shipwreck had been provided for before the Albatross sailed. Therefore, when time came to desert the ship there had been nothing to do but lower the boats.

Prank gazed after his friends as they strode rapidly inland. As they disappeared beyond a distant clump of trees he shrugged.

"Well," he said to the sailors, "they've gone and we're here. I don't imagine any one will bother us, but we'll be on guard. Timothy, you keep your weather eye open for possible callers while Allen and I unload."

The two proceeded untiringly with the work while Timothy scanned the horizon.

Now, it so happened that the sailor paid no attention to the water front. After one brief glance, in which be made sure that there was nothing upon the surface of the water, he confined his attention inland. Therefore, it is only natural that Frank was taken off his feet by surprise when, chancing to look up, he beheld in the harbor a small vessel, to all appearances a submarine, and advancing toward him a dozen or more men, armed with rifles.

Frank staightened up with a cry. Timothy and Allen sprang to his side. Each seized a rifle and loosened the revolvers in their belts.

"Timothy," said Frank severely, "I thought I told you to keep your eyes open."

"I did, sir," replied the sailor, eyeing the approaching men in the utmost surprise. "I'll take my oath there was no submarine there five minutes ago."

"But it must have been in sight," said Frank. "It didn't materialize out of thin air, you know."

"I can't help that," declared Timothy. "It wasn't there, I tell you."

"What's the use of talking like that, man," exclaimed Frank, exasperated. "I tell you it must have been in sight."

Timothy mumbled something to himself, but made no coherent reply.

"Wonder who they are, sir?" said Allen.

"It's too deep for me," said Frank with a shrug. "However, we'll know soon enough. Now, you men keep quiet and let me do the talking. We don't want to have any trouble if we can help it. Chances are they will prove friendly enough. That vessel in the harbor is probably a submarine of some South American government. These men approaching are the officers and crew. We are not at war with any South American country, so there is no reason why we should anticipate trouble."

The newcomers had now approached within hailing distance. At a command from the man who appeared to be the leader they halted. Frank saw that they were all heavily armed. A man stepped forward and shouted:

"Who are you and what do you want here?"

"Castaways!" Frank shouted back. "We're the sole survivors of an American merchant ship."

This reply seemed to lend courage to the others, who, at a command from the leader, advanced boldly.

"Throw down your rifles men," said Frank in a low voice, "but keep your hands on your revolvers. These fellows seem all right, but there is no need taking unnecessary chances."

They stood quietly as the men approached. As they drew nearer, Frank made out that they were indeed a motley crew. Spanish faces -- or South American, to be more exact -- predominated, but there were a few who seemed to be English or

Americans. Also, there were two plainly of African descent and three who seemed to be Chinese or Japanese.

Frank whistled softly to himself.

"If I didn't know the days of pirates are over..." he said, and then shrugged again.

The leader of the party -- a young man, he could not have been more than twenty-four, although he was exceedingly large and powerful looking -- spoke in English. Frank was not wrong when he placed him as an American, though of German descent.

"What's your name?" he demanded of Frank.

"Chadwick," replied Frank quietly. "Frank Chadwick."

"And you say you are castaways?" said the man. "What was your position aboard the ship?"

"Second officer," said Frank

"A merchant ship, you say?"

"Yes."

Frank did not deem it necessary to tell the other that he held a lieutenancy in the British royal navy.

"And you are the sole survivors?" demanded the man.

"So far as I know, yes."

"Good," said the leader of the party. "Then you shall come with us. It may be that you will have brains, in which event your fortune is assured. If no, well, it won't be hard to get rid of you. You'll come with me. Tell your men to follow."

Frank thought quickly. It was plain that he was in danger of some kind though as yet he was unable to tell just what.

"One minute," he said. The others paused.

"Who are you?" the lad demanded.

The other smiled.

"Why, I'm Captain Jack," he said quietly.

"I see," said Frank. "And your ship - a submarine, I note -- a war vessel, it can be plainly seen. What flag does she fly?"

"The black flag," was the smiling reply; "the jolly Roger."

"As I thought," said Frank. "A pirate!"

His hands dropped to his guns.

CHAPTER XVII
A FIGHT

"We are, in South America, all right."

Thus spoke Captain Glenn as he, Jack and Williams proceeded inland after leaving Frank and the two sailors near the shore.

"What makes you think so, Captain?" asked Jack.

"Look at the trees. You find trees like these in no other place besides the tropics. And feel the heat."

"It gets hot other places, sir."

"Not like it does in the tropics. Once you have felt the tropical heat you can't mistake it."

The land in which they now found themselves was thickly covered with big trees. Their foliage was so dense that progress was difficult.

"Good place for snakes, sir," said Williams.

"Fine," agreed Captain Glenn.

"Don't talk about snakes," said Jack with a shudder. "If there is one thing from which I will run a mile it's a snake."

"You won't run a mile from any snake you find around here," said Williams.

"Don't you believe it," declared Jack. "I don't care how small the snake may be, nor how harmless."

"Snakes hereabouts," said Williams, "are neither small nor harmless. That's why I say you won't run a mile from them."

"Surely they won't attack a man," said Jack.

"Ordinarily, no. But when you come upon one unexpectedly he naturally thinks you mean him harm and he acts promptly."

"If a snake ever bit me, that would settle me forever," said Jack.

"Most of these," said Williams, "don't bite. They wrap around a man and crush him to death."

"Look here," said Jack, "are you trying to scare me or what? I don't even like to talk about snakes. Let's drop the subject."

"All right," said Williams, with a smile. "I'm just warning you, that's all."

"Thanks," said Jack dryly.

At this moment there came a sudden exclamation from Captain Glenn, who was slightly ahead. He had just disappeared beyond a clump of trees larger than the rest. Jack stopped stock still. Visions of a snake of monstrous size rose before his eyes.

"Come on," said Williams.

Jack forced himself to follow the other. They darted along the path taken by Captain Glenn and there they came upon the cause of his exclamation. Directly ahead of them lay a broad expanse of water.

"The ocean again," said Captain Glenn. "I should say that we are on an island."

"By Jove!" said Jack, for the moment forgetting all about snakes, "I believe you are right. That means that we are marooned, sir."

"Not necessarily," said Captain Glenn. "We'll head north. We may strike a settlement there."

Accordingly they turned their steps in that direction.

For perhaps two hours they walked without finding signs of human habitation.

"Guess we've gone the wrong way," said Captain Glenn. "We should have turned south. "He glanced at his watch. "We'd better be getting back to the others," he said, "or they will think something has happened to us."

They turned and retraced their steps. For perhaps an hour they walked along and then Jack, who was slightly in advance, stopped suddenly and held up his hand in a warning gesture.

"Someone coming," he whispered.

"Maybe it's a snake," said Williams.

Again Jack shuddered a trifle, but he held his ground. His hands rested on his revolvers.

The sound of creaking twigs reached the ears of the three who stood silently there in the forest. At a sign from Jack, each man got behind a tree and each drew his revolvers. Hardly had they thus screened themselves when half a dozen men burst into view, walking along slowly and laughing.

The men, although they carried rifles, appeared peaceable enough, so Captain Glenn, thinking to bring their long search to an end, stepped forward after they had passed and raised his voice in hello.

Instantly the strangers wheeled about. The man nearest Captain Glenn raised his rifle to his shoulder and his hand pressed the trigger. At that distance a miss would have been impossible. Captain Glenn brought up his own gun, but before he could fire Jack's gun spoke. The man who had covered Captain Glenn dropped to the ground with a wild cry.

Jack's promptness undoubtedly had saved his commander's life.

Saved thus from almost certain death, Captain Glenn quickly sprang behind a tree. Jack and Williams were also sheltered and now held the strangers at a disadvantage. Apparently believing, however, that the hidden men would shoot them down where they stood, one who appeared to be in command of the others raised his voice in a shout. He spoke in English.

"To shelter, men!" he cried.

At the word each man sprang for the nearest tree. Neither Jack, Williams nor Captain Glenn felt impelled to shoot them down in cold blood so all reached shelter safely enough. Jack peered from behind his tree a moment later. As he did so a bullet whizzed by his ear.

"It's a fight," the lad called to Captain Glenn.

"Apparently they don't want us to explain."

Jack sank to the ground and again peered forth. Some distance away he saw a shoulder protruding from behind a tree, Jack raised his rifle and fired.

The man pitched forward into the open with a cry. His cry was echoed by the others, and Jack felt a second bullet whiz overhead.

"Pretty close," the lad muttered, "but it's only four to three now."

For a time all was silent in the forest. Then one of the enemy, more venturesome than the others, darted across the open in an effort to get closer to Jack and his friends.

This time it was the revolver of Williams that spoke and the man dropped in his tracks.

For some time now the enemy showed no disposition to expose himself to the fire of Jack and the others. The forest was as still as death. Jack began to fidget.

"By Jove! This is getting tiresome," he said.

"Must be some way of getting rid of those fellows." He raised his voice and called Captain Glenn. "Cover me," he said. "I'm going to shift my position."

He did not wait for an answer. There were two sharp crashes as he dashed from behind the tree. Jack felt a sting in his left arm and knew that he was not badly hurt. As he jumped behind another tree, he heard Captain Glenn's voice:

"I got him!"

Jack was now so close to the tree behind which Captain Glenn stood that he found he was able to converse with his commander without raising his voice.

"This thing is getting monotonous," he said.

"Exactly," agreed Captain Glenn; "besides which, it is altogether foolish. We haven't anything against these fellows and they surely can't have anything against us."

"You are forgetting the men we have shot, sir," said Jack.

"No, I'm not. That was their own fault. I vote we hold a parley with the remaining two."

"Whatever you say, sir," said Jack.

Captain Glenn raised his voice. "Hello, there!" he cried. "We want to talk to you."

"Talk ahead," said a voice so close that Captain Glenn started.

Apparently one of the enemy had shifted his position. He now was concealed behind the tree next to the captain. Apparently he had been biding his time until the latter should show himself. However, Captain Glenn showed no alarm.

"Then listen," he said. "We have nothing against you fellows. You don't even know us. Therefore why should we fight?"

"Well," said the man behind the next tree, "that's good enough reasoning. I'm willing to call it off any time you say."

"Very good. Drop your gun and step out in the open.'"

"And let you shoot me down? I guess not."

"Come, man, don't be a fool," said Captain Glenn. "We mean you no harm."

"Then you fellows drop your guns and step into the open," was the reply.

"Not much," said Captain Glenn.

The conference was at a deadlock.

"Look here," said Jack, taking a hand in the conversation. "I have a plan that will possibly meet your favor."

"Let's hear it," was the rejoinder.

"We'll throw our rifles into the open and toss out our revolvers. Then you do the same. We'll all step out then."

"Very good," said the hidden man. "Throw yours out first."

Jack hurled his rifle from him and tossed one revolver into the open. Captain Glenn tossed away his revolvers and rifle, and Williams, acquainted with the plan by a shout, followed suit. The unseen men did likewise. Captain Glenn and Williams stepped out. Their adversaries also left their hiding places. Then Jack saw that one of them covered Captain Glenn and Williams with a revolver. Jack smiled, and taking deliberate aim fired. The man's weapon dropped from his hand.

CHAPTER XVIII
CAPTIVES

When "Captain Jack" admitted to Frank that he was a full-fledged pirate, the lad's first thought was to draw his revolvers and open fire. That was why he dropped his hands to his guns following his exclamation of "Pirates."

Timothy and Allen, the two sailors, taking their cue from Frank, also reached for their weapons. Captain Jack, though realizing on the instant what these movements signified, simply smiled.

"I wouldn't, if I were you," he said quietly.

Frank thought better of his plan to fight and dropped his hands to his side again. He, too, smiled.

"Guess you're right," he said quietly.

"Wouldn't do much good, would it?"

"Hardly, with all my men about you. You might get me, and you might not, but they would get you sure."

"I guess I could get you all right," said Frank.

"Maybe so, though I'm pretty handy with a gun. Suppose I can draw quicker and shoot straighter than you or anyone you have seen."

"There is room for argument on that point," said Frank dryly.

"An argument would soon convince you that I am right," was the reply. "However, we will not argue the point now. Nor need we ever argue it if you are reasonable."

"What do you mean by reasonable?" Frank wanted to know.

"Well," said Captain Jack, "truth is I am somewhat short-handed. I lost my first officer in my last battle. Lost half a dozen men along with him. Now you're an officer, though not a military officer. Therefore I can make use of you, if you're open to a proposition."

"Thanks," said Frank quietly, "but I'm not open to a proposition to become a murderer."

"Careful," said Captain Jack, taking a quick step forward. "That kind of talk won't go with me."

"Well, I don't know whether you're one now or not," said Frank, "but you stand in a fair way of becoming one. I have no hankering for piracy."

Captain Jack looked at the lad long and earnestly. Then he said: "Guess I'll make a pirate out of you anyhow. Grab him, men."

Two men leaped upon the lad. Frank's two revolvers flashed out like a streak of lightning and there were two sharp reports. Not for nothing had Jack once declared that Frank was the quickest and best shot he ever hoped to see.

The men who had sprung upon the lad tumbled over. Frank turned to confront the others. As he did so there were two more sharp reports and the lad's two revolvers clattered to the ground. Sharp pains shot through both his wrists and his hands seemed to have been numbed.

The lad turned to where Captain Jack, with two smoking revolvers in his hands, was smiling quietly.

"You reckoned without Captain Jack, you see," said the pirate chief. "Don't worry. You're not hurt. I just felt called upon to shoot away your guns before you annihilated my men here. Now, if you have no objections, I'll have you and your men tied tip and taken aboard the Roger, where you shall be kept until you are wiling to listen to reason."

Timothy and Allen had been deprived of their weapons and at command from

Captain Jack, the three prisoners were securely bound.

"Take them aboard the Roger," instructed the pirate chief with a wave of his hand.

The three captives were led away.

The submarine now had come against the half concealed dock that had caused the castaways such wonderment when they approached the shore. At command of their captors, they leaped to the deck of the submarine and then passed through the conning tower and descended below.

At sight of the interior Frank could not suppress an exclamation of astonishment. The vessel was fitted with the handsomest of appointments. The little cabin into which the three prisoners were led even showed signs of an artistic taste, undoubtedly that of Captain Jack, Frank thought.

"This young pirate certainly has an eye for the beautiful," Frank told himself.

The prisoners once inside the cabin, the captors withdrew and locked the door behind them.

"Well," said Frank, "here we are, men. What are we going to do about it?"

"Nothing we can do, sir," said Allen. "He will probably offer us a chance to join his crew and if we refuse he'll heave us all overboard."

"I'm a f raid he'll have to heave away then," said, Frank, "for I don't think I would make a very good pirate."

"I'd make a better pirate than I would a corpse, sir," declared Timothy, "and this fellow must have made quite a success. Here he is the undisputed owner of a submarine fitted out like a palace; he's his own boss and his prizes he probably distributes among members of the crew. Why, sir, a year of this life and a man would be rich."

"Look here, Timothy," said Frank, "I don't like that kind of talk. Why, man, you talk like you would like to be a pirate."

"Maybe I would, sir. I've thought about it for years. Look at the excitement a man could have."

"Timothy's right, sir," declared Allen. "I'm not hankering for the life of a pirate, but I'm not hankering for a watery grave, either. I don't, know but what I would join if given the chance."

"Look here, men," said Frank, "I'm free to confess that the life of a pirate seems to have its sunny side. I've read a lot of pirate tales and I can remember when I thought I would like to be one. But I know myself and I know you better than you think. When it came to a showdown, you'd balk."

"Well, I'm not sure about that, sir," said Allen..

"I am," declared Frank decisively. "You mark my words, you'll refuse when the time comes."

"Then we'll walk the plank," said Timothy.

"Better to walk the plank with clean hands than to be hanged with the death of innocent persons on your conscience," said Frank.

"We'll see when the times comes," said Allen.

The three were talking of Jack, Captain Glenn and Williams some time later when a hand fumbled with the key in the door. They whirled about quickly, forgetful for the moment that they were helpless in their bonds. A moment later the door swung open and Captain Jack entered, smiling.

"Well, well," he said. "So we're all here, eh? Guess I'll unloosen your hands. I feel that I can handle the whole bunch of you if it's necessary."

He cut the cords that bound them and the three stretched their cramped muscles.

"Now we'll have a little talk," said Captain Jack.

He motioned the three to seats and took a stool himself, near the door, to guard the exit. For the first time Frank took a good look at him.

The pirate chief was perhaps half an inch shorter than Jack Templeton. He was more fully developed, though, as became his years, and had the appearance of being of enormous strength. Frank decided that he was a trifle, though not much, stronger than his chum. He had a pleasant face and smiled continually. There was nothing about him that would label him "pirate."

Captain Jack addressed Frank.

"I've come to ask you to be my first lieutenant," he said.

Frank jumped to his feet.

"I'll see you hanged first," he cried.

Captain Jack smiled calmly.

"No, I don't think you will," he said pleasantly. "I've the whip hand now, you know. If you decline, I shall feel called upon to take stern measures."

"Take them, then," said Frank briefly.

Captain Jack hesitated.

"It seems a pity, too," he said. "You're rather handy with a gun. You could be of great use to me. Now, for example, I have word -- picked up by my wireless station inland -- that a certain ship is about to pass through these waters. It will be loaded with riches. I intend to capture it. I would like to have you lend a hand."

"You've a lot of nerve," said Frank. "You talk about capturing an American ship -- or even a British or French, or of a country allied with the United States -- as though it were nothing."

"Who said it was an American ship or a vessel of an allied nation?" demanded Captain Jack.

"What else could it be?" demanded Frank.

"In this case, it chances to be a German ship," said Captain Jack.

Frank looked incredulous.

"What? Didn't you know the Germans had established a naval base far to the north of this island?" asked Captain Jack. "It's there their raiders put in supplies. There are also a dozen submarines. As a matter of fact though, the Kaiser is a submarine shy. That's the one I 'cut out' about five months ago."

Frank listened to this tale with wide-open eyes.

"If you're fighting the Germans, I'm with you," he said.

Captain Jack shook his head.

"Just when necessary," he said quietly. "This time it chances to be a German I shall attack. I wouldn't hesitate if it were American or British. I am fighting for my own ends only. I am a pirate."

CHAPTER XIX
KAISERLAND

Frank gazed in unconcealed wonder at this young man who thus openly set at naught the laws of nations and of civilization; but he was not greatly surprised at the pirate's announcement that there was a German submarine base in the Atlantic. This had long been suspected in Washington and allied countries, but fast cruisers sent to scour the waters had been unable to find the hiding place.

Captain Jack continued:

"You see, I'm not asking you to join me under false pretenses. I could tell you I am fighting Germany, attack a German ship and you would believe me; but that is not the truth. In fact, I hesitate even to attack this German ship. Should my hiding place be discovered, the Germans would make short work of me."

"So would American or British warships," said Frank.

"I'm not so sure. If pursued by them I would appeal to the Germans for aid. They would welcome me as a kindred spirit -- they are no better than pirates, you know."

"Oh, I know it, all right," Frank agreed. "In fact, I have found that they are not as good as most pirates, though, I am not what you would call well acquainted with the pirate family. By the way, where are we?"

Captain Jack considered.

"I guess there is no need for me to remain silent on that point," he said at last. "There is little likelihood that you will be able to reveal my hiding place. This island, to give it the name of the Germans who hold forth here, is Kaiserland. It is out of the regular channel of navigation from South America and is uncharted. I stumbled upon it by accident.

"Shipwrecked, as were you, with fifty men from a South American freight ship, we dragged ourselves ashore here. We discovered the German base while hunting signs of human habitation. It was then I conceived the idea of seizing one of the German vessels. My men were with me -- it was a rough lot we carried on that freight ship. I seemed to have more brains -- or you can call it imagination -- than the rest, so I became the leader as a natural result.

"I won't burden you with the details of how we captured the submarine. The best proof that we succeeded, however, is that you are board it right now. I had all kinds of men among my followers, even the wireless operator. He rigged up a wireless station farther inland. There, I picked up many messages the world would be glad to hear."

"Did you ever stop to think," said Frank," of what benefit you could be to the United States and her allies?"

"I have," returned Captain Jack, "but I have concluded that I can be of more use to myself. So far I have sunk but three vessels and in each case I have set passengers and crew safely adrift in the regular channel, where they were sure to be picked up. There will be some great tales when they reach home. They probably will blame their misfortune on the Germans.

"But there is nothing I could do for the United States now without inviting my own destruction. I have gone beyond the pale, and the punishment for piracy, you know, is death. But come, I am wasting time. Again I ask will you be my first lieutenant and join me in my dash after this German raider."

Frank considered deeply for long minutes. At last he said: "I cannot accept your offer to become a pirate, but I will do this: I will take part in your attack on the German, for I consider any German engaged in this war beyond the pale of civilization. If it is necessary to become a pirate to help win this war, then I will become a pirate, always remembering myself that I shall break none of the laws of nations and that I shall take every effort to succor the unfortunate."

"Good!" exclaimed Captain Jack. "Well spoken!"

"But," continued Frank, "I want you to understand that I wish no part of the prize and that my association with you ends when the German raider has been disposed of."

"Very good!" declared Captain Jack. "So be it. And your men here, I take it, are of the same mind?"

"We are, sir," said Timothy and Allen in a single voice.

They seemed to have lost all desire to become pirates in reality.

"You may consider yourselves at liberty, then," said Captain Jack, with a wave of his hand. "By the way," this to Frank, "do you know anything of the mechanism of a submarine?"

"A trifle," said Frank quietly. "I neglected to tell you that I hold a lieutenant's commission in the British navy."

"What!" cried Captain Jack, who could scarcely believe his ears.

"Exactly," said Frank, "and as such I have seen considerable active service beneath the sea as well as upon its surface."

"So much the better," declared Captain Jack. "You will be all the more valuable. I need not fear to trust my ship in your hands."

At this moment there came sounds of confusion from above.

"Something wrong," said Captain Jack, and dashed away.

Frank and the two sailors followed more slowly. Captain Jack met them at the foot of the ladder that led on deck. He was laughing.

"Nothing serious," he said. "Half a dozen of my men encountered three strangers back on the island and there was a fight. Seems the strangers had the better of the encounter, killing two of my, men and wounding two more. Through some sort of a truce the strangers agreed to accompany my men here, although they seem to have had the advantage."

Captain Jack made as if to mount the ladder. Frank stayed him.

"One minute," he said. "Chances are your captives are friends of mine, my commander, and the fourth officer of the Albatross. Don't worry," as Captain Jack laid a hand to his revolver, "they are with me in anything I do. But I thought we could have a little fun with them. Take charge of them like the pirate chief you are and tell them you are leaving their fate in the hands of your first officer."

"By Jove! Good!" cried Captain Jack, and he climbed on deck.

Frank led the way into what he made out was the pirate chief's cabin and unceremoniously took possession.

A few moments later several figures descended the ladder and approached the cabin. Frank caught Jack's voice.

"I was a fool to let these fellows get the upper hand," he said. "We had the advantage back there in the forest and threw it away. No telling what they will do with us. Make us walk the plank, maybe."

Frank got to his feet as Jack, Williams and Captain Glenn, closely followed by Captain Jack, entered the little cabin. Jack espied him on the instant.

"Hello, Frank," he said, with a rueful smile.

"So they got you, too, eh?"

"No, they didn't get me," replied Frank, "but it seems we have got you, all right."

"What's that?" demanded Jack, believing he had not heard aright.

"I say," declared Frank, "that we've got you. I'm second in command of this pirate crew and I don't want you to forget it. You will address me with civility."

"What's the joke?" asked Jack.

"No joke," returned Frank. "I'm the first officer of this submarine, and Captain

Jack -- that's your captor -- has left it to me to pronounce sentence on the men who have killed two of our good pirates and wounded two others."

"So you've joined the pirates?" said Jack, with a smile. "All right, we await the sentence. What is it? Walk the plank?"

"No," said Frank, "the sentence is that you become members of our pirate crew."

"What," said Jack in mock seriousness, and supposing of course that Frank was joking, "me a pirate? I guess not."

"Either that," said Frank, "or you shall be bound and securely guarded until we have returned from an imminent cruise."

"Look here, Chadwick," interposed Captain Glenn at this point, "all this probably is very funny and all that; but tell us the joke so we can laugh too."

"I'm telling you that it's no joke," replied Frank. "I am asking you whether, for the moment, you will all become pirates and fare forth with Captain Jack and myself in search of adventure, riches and Germans."

"Germans?" said Jack, pricking up his ears.

"Sure, we'll fare forth with almost any one in search of Germans. Explain, Frank."

"First," said Frank, "I want you to meet Captain Jack, a true pirate. Captain Jack, my friend and chum, Jack Templeton."

"Seems we've both got a regular name, anyhow, doesn't it," said Jack Templeton, as he shook hands with Captain Jack.

"It does," returned the latter with a grin.

The two took stock of each other, each realizing in the moment their hands met that before him stood an antagonist worthy of his steel.

Frank introduced the others. Then he explained the situation.

"Now do you think I have done right to join the expedition?" he asked.

"You have done right, yes," said Jack slowly, weighing each word, "if you are sure you can trust our Captain Jack, here."

Captain Jack was on his feet with an angry gleam in his eyes, but Jack did not quail. Before the look in the young Englishman's eye, the pirate chief stepped back. Then he looked the lad squarely in the face and extended his hand.

"You've my word that I will play square," he said quietly, and added half ruefully, "The word of a pirate!"

"I accept it!" said Jack, and grasped the hand.

CHAPTER XX
THE ATTACK

Jack now explained to the others how he and his two companions had encountered the pirate forces in the forest.

"So after I fired at the treacherous pirate," he concluded, "we framed up an agreement to come along with those able to walk. It's true we held the upper hand at that moment, but we were strangers in a strange land, so to speak, and we needed help. Besides, the man didn't explain that they were pirates."

The attack upon the German raider was set for the next night when a messenger from the wireless station in the woods apprised Captain Jack of the approximate hour at which the German ship would pass a certain point.

That night the friends spent aboard the submarine at the bottom of the harbor. The fact that the vessel submerged with the coming of darkness accounted for its sudden appearance from nowhere the morning the castaways landed.

The following day was spent quietly ashore. Jack and Frank talked over the decision they had reached to join the pirate forces against the Germans and each felt certain that they were acting wisely and well.

"And what will Captain Jack do with us when we return?" asked Frank.

Jack shrugged his shoulders.

"It's hard to say," he replied. "However, there is no use worrying. Let tomorrow take care of itself."

"Well," said Frank, "I'm going to secrete a couple of revolvers. I'm not going to be shot down after this piece of work is done."

"Right," Jack agreed. "I'll do the same if I can and I'll pass the word to Williams, Captain Glenn and the sailors."

Thus it was arranged.

It was two hours before dark the following day when, with Captain Jack at the wheel and the Roger running submerged, the start was made to intercept the German raider.

"There is probably no one near now," said Captain Jack, "but I am running submerged because I think it is foolish to take chances."

"Will you have to submerge to launch your torpedoes?" asked Frank.

"I will in this case. Here's my plan: I want to hit the German in a vulnerable and not a vital spot. I don't want her to sink, but I do want to damage her so badly that the crew will abandon her. Then I can go aboard and get whatever I want."

"I don't think so much of the second part of the program," said Jack. "It would be all right, of course, if whatever is found was to be used by nations at war with Germany, but by a --"

"Pirate," interposed Captain Jack, with a slight smile. "Why don't you say it? You don't need to spare my feelings. I'm perfectly hardened, I assure you."

"Well, I don't like the word," said Jack. "It has an ugly sound."

Captain Jack's face flushed and his hands clenched, but lie said nothing.

With the coming of nightfall, Captain Jack ordered the automatic pumps to work, and as the water was forced from the tanks the submarine came to the surface. Captain Jack motioned Jack and Frank to follow him on deck.

The night was still. There was hardly a ripple on the sea.

"How much farther do we go?" asked Frank.

Captain Jack glanced at his pocket compass and then at his wrist watch. "If I've calculated correctly," he replied, "we shall reach our station within two hours. The German should be along within the next sixty minutes. You fellows wait here a minute. I'm going below."

He left the two lads alone on deck, which was only a few feet above the level of the ocean. The conning tower closed behind him. The same thought flashed through the minds of both lads, but Frank gave it expression.

"Wonder if he's going to submerge and let us be washed away?" he asked.

Jack shrugged his shoulders again -- a habit he had.

"We should have thought of that sooner," he said. "It's too late now. We'll have to wait and see."

But the vessel remained on an even keel and directly the conning tower opened and Captain Jack emerged.

"Think I was going to run from under you?" he asked, with a smile.

"Such a thought had struck us, to tell the truth about it," said Jack.

"Don't worry," said Captain Jack, and added grimly, "at least not until this night's work is over."

Neither Jack nor Frank felt called upon to reply to this remark. For some moments the three stood in silence scanning the black expanse of water as the submarine nosed gently along. Then Captain Jack broke the silence.

"Let's go below," he said.

Two hours later Captain Jack again went on deck. He motioned to Frank to follow him. In spite of the fact that Captain Glenn, a man of proven experience, was aboard and that Jack had ranked above Frank on the Albatross, the pirate chief still held to Frank for his first officer.

"Chadwick," he said, "I shall leave the handling of the craft to you when we go into action. I shall be busy with the torpedoes. Your friend Templeton I will post at the periscope to get the range."

"Very good, sir," said Frank, saluting as though he were aboard a ship of war and serving under a military officer.

Captain Jack poked his head down the hatchway and called to Jack, who was stationed there:

"Stop the engines, Mr. Templeton."

"Very good, sir," was Jack's reply.

The submarine's progress was stopped. She rode gently on the waves now, moving only with the tide. Captain Jack and Frank scanned the distant and dark horizon for some sight of the raider.

"She'll come dark," said Captain Jack. "She won't dare show a light for fear of being picked up; and I don't dare use my searchlight for the same reason. She should be here now."

"Plans may have been changed," said Frank briefly.

"That's so, and still I hardly believe that is it. They were flashed, you know, to a point on the South American coast, from which they are relayed to Berlin. The German government, in spite of the efforts of the Allies to prevent it, is still informed of every move this fleet in far-off waters makes."

"It seems incredible," declared Frank.

"Nevertheless it's true. Is it any wonder a fellow who is playing as safe as he can would lean toward Germany rather than the Allies. Also, to my mind, it seems to be a case of Germany being the under dog and my sympathies are naturally with that animal."

"It isn't that," said Frank. "The Allies, the United States included, are not in this war to thrash any one. They're in this war to make the world safe to live in. So long as Prussian militarism exists, there will be no peace and no safety for any man, woman, or child in any country."

"You may be right," said Captain Jack, "and you may not be. Fact is, I haven't bothered to give the matter much thought. My business has to do with making money, and more particularly, at this moment, of catching sight of the German at the earliest possible moment. She will come close in this darkness before we are able to see her, and fast work will be necessary then. We can't make much time in this submarine, you know, and if we are not careful she'll run away from us."

"Trouble is," said Frank, "that she may be some distance away when she passes this point. You can't tell exactly where she'll pass."

"That's it," said Captain Jack. "That's what I am worrying about."

"Well," said Frank, "she -- what's that?"

He broke off suddenly. A large shape loomed up in the darkness, some distance away.

"The raider!" cried Captain Jack. "Quick! Below!"

He sprang for the hatchway and dashed to the torpedo tubes. Frank scrambled madly after him and took the wheel from the helmsman with such promptness as to send the man sprawling.

"Get the range, Jack!" he cried.

Jack, with his eye to the periscope, called out sharply:

"Number three, torpedo."

Captain Jack himself sprang to the tube.

"Hold her as she is!" cried Jack. "Fire!"

Captain Jack, instead of touching off the torpedo, suddenly stepped back.

"I'm liable to sink her, and I don't want to do that," he said.

"Shoot, man!" cried Jack. "Shoot or she'll get away."

"Well, there is no use angering the Germans for nothing," said Captain Jack. "They'll start a search for me. If I can't get the rich booty aboard there is no reason for me to fire. No, I'll wait until some other night, when I can be sure the shot will go where I intend it and merely cripple her."

With a sudden angry cry, Jack hurled himself forward. Captain Jack had stepped back some distance from the tube. He leaped, forward as he realized the lad's intention. But he was too late.

There was a slight metallic click; that was all.

The torpedo sped on its errand of destruction. Jack whirled about in time to meet the attack of the pirate chief. They grappled and went to the deck with a crash.

CHAPTER XXI
JACK VS. JACK

Diabolical anger showed upon the face of Captain Jack as he grappled with the young Englishman. The pirate chief held the advantage when the two came together, for he had the impetus of his advance behind him, while Jack was off his balance when they grappled. Therefore Captain Jack was uppermost when they struck the deck.

Three members of the pirate crew -- all that were near at that moment -- sprang forward to lend a hand to their leader. Then Frank took charge of the situation. He produced two revolvers with a single movement. Williams did likewise. Captain Glenn, always a sailor, sprang to the wheel and put the submarine back on an even keel -- she had been staggering when Frank released his hold. The sailors Timothy and Allen were in another part of the vessel at the moment.

"Stand back!" cried Frank, and the pirates halted in their tracks.

Frank covered them with his two revolvers.

"Get their guns," the lad instructed Williams.

The latter obeyed and soon the three pirates were helpless.

In the meantime, Jack and Captain Jack, closely locked, were struggling for mastery. Williams advanced to lend Jack a hand, but Frank motioned him back. He had no fear of the outcome despite the fact that Captain Jack seemed to have all the advantage.

"Let 'em alone, Williams!" the lad cried. "A thrashing will do the pirate good; and he's about to get it."

Williams stood back, but he and Frank both held their automatics ready for instant use, for they were determined to see fair play.

Jack was still underneath, but be had thrown both powerful arms around the neck of the pirate captain and the latter, who had now got to his knees, was struggling to break this hold. Jack held on grimly.

Suddenly Jack braced his feet against one side of the narrow corridor, and still lying on his back, heaved mightily. The pirate chief, powerful man though he was, went sailing in the air and his head struck the opposite wall with a resounding crack.

Jack released his hold and sprang to his feet

The shock had momentarily stunned Captain Jack and Jack stood back, waiting for the pirate to regain his senses. The man staggered to his feet, brushed his hand across his face and then glared at Jack.

"A very pretty trick," he exclaimed, "but you won't catch me napping again."

He sprang toward Jack and aimed a vicious blow at the lad's face with his right fist. Jack stepped nimbly aside and the blow went wide. Before the pirate could recover his balance, Jack struck him a heavy blow under the right ear. A less powerful man would have gone down under the force of it, but Captain Jack simply shook his head angrily and turned sharply to renew the attack. Nevertheless, this time he advanced with greater caution.

For several moments the two stood at arm's length and sparred. In this style of fighting, however, the young Englishman had all the better of it and after he had landed several blows upon the pirate's face and body, the latter rushed into a clinch.

Captain Jack had lost his first pangs of anger and was fighting more coolly and carefully now. He realized after a few minutes that he had met his match, and, he wasn't sure as yet, but, perhaps, his superior.

As the two struggled in each other's embrace, each seeking an advantage without presenting an opening, Jack Templeton smiled and spoke.

"I've got you, Captain Jack," he said, "but I am ready to cry quits any time you give the word."

Captain Jack made no reply, but only tried the harder to encircle Jack's neck with his right arm.

Suddenly Jack freed his right arm, which had been pressed close to his body by the pirate's left, and brought his fist up under Captain Jack's chin. It was a powerful short-arm blow and the pirate chief staggered back. Jack gave him no time to li ft his guard, but bored in.

"Crack! Crack!"

Right and left, with all Jack's strength behind them, struck the pirate, the first between the eyes and the second on the chin. Captain Jack floundered back across the corridor.

Jack stopped in his tracks; then, pivoting on his heel, he shot out his right with all his power. Captain Jack, struck again squarely upon the point of the chin, crumpled tip without a word and lay still.

Jack stepped back and surveyed his fallen foe.

"Easier than I thought it would be," he said quietly. "Had he known anything of boxing there might have been a different story to tell."

Frank stepped forward and took his friend's hand.

"You're some scrapper, all right," he said, "but what are we going to do now?"

"Well," said Jack, "we seem to be in command of this submarine. I vote that we appropriate it for the British navy."

"Or the American navy," added Frank.

"Whichever you say," said Jack.

"In the meantime," said Williams dryly, "it might be well to tie up our pirate commander."

"Right you are," said Jack. "Frank, you see to that, will you? I want to go on deck and see whether my torpedo struck home."

Without waiting for a reply he mounted the ladder.

Frank turned to look about for strong cord with which to bind the pirate captain. As he did so he was startled by a cry from Captain Glenn at the wheel. He had replaced his revolvers, but now his hands dropped to them. Before he could draw, however, strong hands drew him back. Williams also was suddenly attacked from behind.

Captain Glenn released the wheel, but before he could produce a weapon, he found himself looking down the barrel of a shining automatic held by a member of the pirate crew.

What had happened was this: While Jack had struggled with the pirate chief, several members of the crew had watched the struggle from the safety of the darkened corridor. They had made no effort to interfere while Frank and Williams stood guard with their revolvers, but when Jack went on deck and Frank and Williams put away their weapons they crept close and sprang when the moment was propitious.

Frank struggled desperately, but hands held him tight. So with Williams. A moment later both were securely bound, and the pirates then gave their attention to Captain Glenn, who also was safely tied up.

While these proceedings were going on Captain Jack opened his eyes. He took in the situation clearly and got to his feet. He approached Frank.

"It seems," he said quietly, "that we have resumed our former status. Once more I am the captor and you are my prisoners. Where's Templeton?"

"On deck, Captain," said one of the pirates.

"Good!" said Captain Jack. "Four of you station yourselves at the ladder there and grab him when he comes down."

The pirates followed instructions. To Frank Captain Jack said:

"I would advise you not to cry out when he descends. If you do it may be necessary to shoot him."

Frank realized the value of this reasoning and promised to say nothing. Williams and Captain Glenn also signified their intention to remain quiet.

Meanwhile, Jack, on deck, scanned the sea through the blackness in an effort to pick up the German raider if she still remained afloat. As his eyes became accustomed to the darkness, he saw what he believed was a mass of wreckage some distance away. Gradually the shape in the water became more distinct.

It was indeed the wreckage of the German raider that Jack beheld there in the darkness.

"Pretty good shooting, Jack, old boy," the lad told himself. "Can't tell whether the crew went down or has made off in the boats. However, there is nothing we can do for them. Guess I'd better be getting back below."

He descended the ladder.

As he stepped from the bottom rung, many hands seized him from behind and he was carried to the deck. Jack struck out with both hands and kicked with both feet. Grunts told him that several of these blows had found their mark.

But the odds against him were too great. Gradually he was borne back and at last, it seemed to the lad, many men sat on his chest. He heard the voice of Captain Jack:

"Bind him securely, men."

Jack quit struggling and lay still.

Two minutes later he was securely bound and permitted to stand. Captain Jack grinned at him.

"He laughs best who laughs last," he quoted, with a smile.

"So he does," Jack agreed, "but I don't think this is the last laugh."

"Well," said Captain Jack, "you've been on deck, did your torpedo go home?"

"It did," said Jack quietly.

"That means," said Captain Jack, "that I probably shall have trouble with the Germans on Kaiserland. They won't rest until they clear up the mystery. I ought to have you shot."

"Suit yourself," said Jack briefly.

For a moment the pirate chief eyed the lad angrily. Then he said:

"I'll decide on your punishment later. Meanwhile, we'll get back to the island."

CHAPTER XXII
ESCAPE

It was the afternoon following return of the submarine to the harbor of, Kaiserland. Frank, Jack, Captain Glenn and Williams found themselves the center of a body of armed men. They were marching inland.

Frank hailed Captain Jack, who marched near the head of the procession.

"Where are you taking us?" he demanded.

"I'd thought about turning you over to the Germans," replied Captain Jack, dropping back and falling in alongside Frank.

"I guess you won't do that," said Frank.

"Why won't I?"

"Because it wouldn't be healthy for you. The Germans would think you had a hand in the sinking of the raider."

"Well, you're right, I guess, so I won't turn you over to the Germans right now. But I've a nice little place away back in the forest, where I think you will be safe enough until it is time for me to leave this island for good."

"So you have decided to give up piracy, eh?" asked Frank.

"Almost. One more good haul and I'll have enough to keep me in plenty the rest of my days. My men, too, will be provided for. Why should we keep this up, when we are sure to be caught sooner or later?"

"I'm glad you've seen the light; but if you'll take my advice, you'll quit this business without waiting for the next haul, as you term it."

Captain Jack shook his head.

"No," he said, "I'm decided on that."

"By the way," said Frank, "where is this place you are taking us?"

"Northern end of the island," said Captain Jack. "Most of my men are there. They'll guard you safe enough. In fact, I may say that the place I am taking you is my headquarters. There I have my office, my wireless apparatus and many other things. Oh, yes, you'll be safe enough there."

"Suit yourself," said Frank, "only remember that some day you will answer for your crimes. By the way, what have you done with our two sailor?"

"Done with them?" repeated Captain Jack. "I haven't done anything with them. They have joined my band."

"Is that so?" returned Frank. "I was afraid of it. They told me they would join if you gave them a chance, but I didn't believe it. Oh, well, I guess they will swing along with the rest of you when the time comes."

Captain Jack left Frank's side and moved to the head of the procession again. He smiled at Jack as he passed. Apparently he bore no grudge for the way the lad had maltreated him aboard the submarine.

"This Captain Jack is a pretty decent sort of a pirate," said Jack. "Too bad he won't run straight."

"Decent or not," said Captain Glenn, "a pirate's a pirate, and if we can manage to get out of his clutches it's up to us to do it."

"Right, sir," agreed Williams. "If we can get a couple of guns apiece and get clear, I'll guarantee we can make considerable trouble for Mr. Pirate before he nabs us again."

"We'll take advantage of the first opportunity that presents itself," said Frank, "no matter how small the chance of success may seem."

"And then what?" Jack wanted to know.

"We'll let the future take care of itself," said Captain Glenn quietly.

Darkness was falling when Captain Jack announced that they were nearing the end of their journey.

"I'm glad of that," said Frank. "Hope there will be a good supper ready."

"Don't you fret," laughed the pirate chief, "I'm not one of those old-fashioned pirates who starved his captives to death."

"I'm glad to hear that, Captain," declared Jack.

"Hope you don't fatten us up too much before the feast, though."

Again Captain Jack laughed, but he made no reply.

Fifteen minutes later the four prisoners made out in the semi-darkness what appeared to be a large stockade.

"Afraid of Indians, Captain?" asked Frank.

"No; Germans," was the response. "We built that wall the better to defend ourselves if we are attacked."

"You're far-seeing, at all events," declared Jack.

Half a dozen men advanced from the enclosure to meet Captain Jack and his party. The pirate chief saluted them and they greeted him cordially.

From the top of a wooded building inside the enclosure Frank made out a large wireless aerial.

"Captain Jack is a modern pirate, all right," the lad told himself.

"Send Jackson to me," ordered Captain Jack, as he followed his prisoners into the large wooden building.

A man left the room, but reappeared a few moments later, followed by a man of extremely large stature.

"Jackson," said Captain Jack, and indicated the four captives with a sweeping gesture, "these men are prisoners and I want them well guarded. You'll lock them up in the strong room and post guards outside. You will keep the keys to the door yourself. No one must enter without my permission. Do you understand?"

"Yes, sir," replied Jackson.

"Good. Take them away, then."

Jackson motioned the prisoners to precede him through the door. As Frank passed out, Captain Jack called:

"I'll do myself the pleasure of calling on you tomorrow."

The big building in which the prisoners found themselves was partitioned off into a number of rooms. As they passed a door, Jack heard a faint clicking.

"Wireless room there," he said aloud.

Frank nodded in the half light.

"That's where Captain Jack gets all his tips," he said.

At the end of a long hall, the prisoners brought up against a stout door. Jackson advanced, produced a key and flung the door open.

"This will be your prison," he said. "You will find no windows, but I will provide you with sufficient candles and matches. It will do no good to try to escape as the door is of the stoutest oak; but even if you did batter it down you would find guards without and the noise would arouse the rest of us. You will find bunks inside."

"Are you going to leave us tied up like this?" demanded Frank, extending his bound hands.

"Why, I guess there is no need of that," said Jackson.

He produced a knife and cut the cords. The prisoners entered the large room. Jackson drew half a dozen candles and a quantity of matches from his pocket. These he gave to Jack.

"Make yourselves as comfortable as possible," he said.

He shut the door and locked it from the outside.

With the candles lighting up the interior of the room, the prisoners surveyed their surroundings. The room contained half a dozen hard chairs and as many bunks. There was a single table. That was all.

"Not a very presentable place, if you ask me," declared Frank.

"But a first class prison," was Williams' comment.

All that night and the next day the prisoners remained there without sight of a human face save that of Jackson who himself brought them their meals. Captain Jack failed to keep his promise to call.

"I'm getting tired of this place," declared Frank, as he made ready for bed the following night.

"Same here," said Jack, "but what are we going to do about it?"

The answer came from an unexpected source.

The stout door creaked slightly. A moment later the head of the sailor Allen appeared within. He laid a finger to his lips and uttered a warning.

"S-h-sh!" as he entered the room. Timothy appeared behind him.

From their pockets the two sailors produced twelve Colt automatics, loaded, and an extra supply of ammunition. They motioned the prisoners to help themselves.

"But why all this?" demanded Frank in a low voice. "I thought you fellows had become pirates."

"So did we, sir," whispered Timothy, "but when we found they had locked you up here we changed our minds."

"How'd you get in?"

"Well," said Allen, grinning, "we were put on watch. Jackson appeared a few minutes ago to see that everything was 0. K. Timothy, here, bumped him over the head with the butt of his gun. Then we took the key and opened the door. That's all, sir."

"You've done well," said Captain Glenn. "The next thing is to get out of here."

"No difficulty there," said Allen. "Everybody is asleep."

"Let's go, then," said Frank.

Armed with two revolvers apiece, the six left the room quietly. They were not accosted as they made their way through the darkened building. They passed noiselessly into the stockade, but there they found that the heavy gates were barred.

"Nothing to do but go over the top," whispered Frank.

Jack boosted Frank up. Sitting astride the wall, Frank lent the others a helping hand and soon they were over the wall.

"Guess it's up to us to lose ourselves in the jungles," said Frank dryly. "Come on."

The others followed. Five minutes later they were out of sight from the stockade. They plunged into the darkness among the great trees.

CHAPTER XXIII
CAPTURING THE WIRELESS STATION

Morning. As the first faint streak of light came streaming over the treetops and dimly lighted the forest itself, Frank stirred his five sleeping comrades with the toe of his boot.

"Time to get up," he said in a low voice to each.

Since midnight the lad had stood guard. There was little likelihood, the friends knew, that their escape would be discovered before morning, but it had been decided that watch should be kept nevertheless, Jack had stood watch until midnight, after which Frank took up the vigil.

With all upon their feet now, Frank called a council of war.

"We've got to decide what to do," he said.

We've come away without as much as a bite to eat. It's likely that we can rustle up something in the forest, also water to quench our thirsts, but I'm in favor of more substantial food."

"What do you suggest, then?" asked Williams.

"Well," said Frank, "it's certain that our absence will be discovered soon after daylight. Naturally they'll make a search for us, because Captain Jack will not feel easy while we are at large. I figure that he will scout the forest with the bulk of his men, leaving the so-called fort lightly guarded. My plan would be to work back toward the enemy, and when we hear them coming take shelter in the tops of these big trees. When they have gone by, we'll come down and go to the fort. There we'll get all the chow we want."

"That's not a bad plan," decided Jack, "but you haven't carried it far enough, Frank."

"What do you mean?" asked Frank.

"Well," said Jack, "we can also take charge of the wireless room. You know I have had some experience in wireless telegraphy. Maybe we can pick up an American ship of war."

"By George! A good idea!" exclaimed Captain Glenn. "But we can't tell them where we are."

"That's true, too," said Jack, "but we can fix our location so closely that they should be able to find us."

"It's worth trying, anyhow," declared Williams.

"All right, then," said Jack. "We may as well be on the move."

Jack took the lead and they retraced the route they had traversed in their flight through the night.

It seemed to all members of the party that they had walked for hours, when Jack suddenly called a halt.

"Thought I heard voices," he said. "Guess we'd better play safe. Our place now is up in the trees."

He scanned the big trees near by. A short distance away were two even larger than the rest. Their branches were so thick that Jack felt sure they would form a perfect screen.

"Let's climb," he said.

Jack clambered up the nearest tree. Captain Glenn and Williams followed him. Frank, Timothy and Allen swung themselves into the other. There, high up among the branches, they sat quietly, waiting.

Their patience was rewarded at last. An hour later, peeping from his hiding place, Frank saw the familiar figure of Captain Jack. To right and left his men were beating the brush in an effort to find the fugitives. Each man carried a rifle ready for instant use.

Frank smiled to himself.

"You want to look up and not down," he said softly.

Captain Jack was exhorting his men to greater pains.

"Don't miss an inch of the ground," he shouted. "We're bound to find them sooner or later. Five hundred dollars in gold to the man who discovers them first. Keep working, men, and be careful."

The searchers passed directly beneath the trees in which the fugitives were hiding. It would have been an easy matter for Frank or any of the others to have killed Captain Jack and several of his men with a single volley, but none could bring himself to shoot down a man in cold blood. Besides, a single shot would have precipitated a battle, and all the fugitives knew that their best chance of safety lay in avoiding discovery.

Directly beneath the tree in which Frank was hiding, Captain Jack paused and lighted his pipe. Then, with a word to his men, he passed on.

The fugitives in the trees almost held their breath for fear they would betray their hiding place. For an hour after the pirates had passed they remained perfectly motionless, fearing that one or more men had perhaps lagged behind.

Then Jack slid down the tree and the others followed him.

"Now for the fort," cried Jack.

The six made off through the woods as fast as possible. Just beyond the trees at the edge of the clearing in which the fort stood, Jack, who had appointed himself commander of the expedition, halted.

"I don't know whether the gate is locked or not," he said. "Chances are, though, that it's not. Neither can we tell how many men are within or whether they are on guard. I believe, however, that we will be safe enough if we cross the clearing at a run. They won't hardly be looking for us to come back."

"You're right, Templeton," said Captain Glenn.

"Let's be moving, then," said Frank impatiently. "Ready?" asked Jack, looking the others over.

Every man held an automatic ready for action in each hand.

"All ready," said Williams.

"Then follow me!"

Jack dashed from the forest straight toward the fort. Spreading out a trifle, so as to make as poor marks as possible should they be discovered, the others dashed after him.

No one opposed their advance across the open and they reached the gate without discovery here they halted a minute. Then Jack laid his shoulder to the gate and pushed.

The gate flew open and the six rushed inside.

At the door to the fort itself stood a single figure. He took one look at the men bearing down on him, fired at them without taking aim and dashed inside.

"Quick! Before he locks the door!" shouted Jack.

He leaped forward and succeeded in putting his foot in the door before the man could close it.

"Lend me a hand here and force the door!" the lad cried.

Captain Glenn and Williams threw their weight against it. The door was flung open. Jack ducked as he ran in and it was well that he did so.

There was a flash and a bullet sped over his head. Before the man could fire again, Jack had closed with him and reversing his revolver quickly, brought the butt down on the man's head with all his force. The pirate toppled to the floor.

Jack jumped across the inert body. Frank was at his heels.

At the far end of the main room four men barred progress. Frank's revolvers spoke sharply twice as he ran forward and two men dropped. Jack felt a twinge of pain in his left side as he advanced and realized that he had been hit. He did not falter, however.   His own revolvers spoke and the door to the next room was closed.

The room in which the six now found themselves was the main room in the fort. Doors led off from three directions, one, as Jack knew, to the wireless room.

"Guard the doors!" shouted Jack. "Shoot the first head you see!"

The others asked no questions but took their positions.

"Frank," said Jack, "we want to get into that wireless room. I don't know how many men there may be in there. I'm going to break in the door. You cover me."

Frank advanced and took position behind Jack.

The latter drew back a bit, then dashed at the door. It was of stout oak, this door, but beneath Jack's weight, the lock was shattered.

As the lad plunged head foremost into the room, there were several sharp flashes as revolvers spat at him. A bullet plowed through his left shoulder, but he took no heed, nor did it even stop his rush.

At one side of the room stood three men with leveled revolvers. Into these Jack pitched headlong before they could fire again.

On the opposite side of the room stood two more men. Frank, dashing into the room right behind Jack, opened on these with his revolvers. One dropped before he could return the lad's fire, but a bullet from the second man's revolver grazed the lobe of Frank's right ear. But the man never fired again. Another bullet from Frank's automatic brought him to the floor.

Jack, when he pitched in among the three men, fired twice - once with each revolver. The enemy also fired, but their nerves were so unsteady at this unexpected rush that the bullets went wild.

Fighting was too close now to bring revolvers into play, so Jack used his automatics as clubs.

A man toppled over before a powerful blow. Frank now came to Jack's aid.

He poked his revolver into one man's back and commanded:

"Hands up!"

The command was obeyed on the instant. At the same moment the other pirate, now clenched in Jack's powerful arms, cried out:

"I surrender."

Jack released him. The two lads were now undisputed masters of the field. They returned to the other room, pushing their captives out ahead of them.

CHAPTER XXIV
AN "S. 0. S." CALL

"By Jove, Jack," said Captain Glenn, as the lads and their prisoners appeared, "that's what I call quick action. How many more men do you suppose there are here now?"

"I don't know," was the lad's reply. "I'll ask our friends here." He shook the man nearest him, roughly. "How many more men in the fort?" he demanded.

This prisoner chanced to be the wireless operator, so he spoke English.

"No more, sir, I am sure," he said fearfully.

"Don't you lie to me," said Jack sternly.

"I'm not lying," protested the operator. "Ask Pedro there, if you do not believe me."

Jack whirled on the second captive.

"How many?" he demanded of the South American.

"No more, senor," was the man's quaking response.

"Maybe not," said Jack, "but if I find you have not told me the truth, it will be the worse for you. Captain Glenn, will you have these fellows tied up? Then the rest of you stand guard at the door. See if you can repair that outer door. Captain Jack and the others will be back some time and we don't want to be taken by surprise. I'll have a little session with the wireless."

"How about your wounds?" asked Williams.

"Scratches," replied Jack briefly. "I don't have time to bother with them now. I'll have 'em fixed up later. Now you fellows do as I tell you."

The others recognized Jack's authority. The prisoners were bound and locked in another room. Captain Glenn and Williams stood guard at the door, that they might not be surprised by the return of the pirates.

Frank started a tour of inspection with the an announcement that he would gather whatever firearms he could find and make sure there were no pirates in the fort. He also bound up the men who had been wounded in the fighting. The dead men he laid on cots until such time as they could be given burial.

Jack took the operator's seat in the wireless room and adjusted the receiver to his head. Then he began to experiment with the key. Directly sharp flashes of light from the aerial without showed that be was flashing messages into space.

For perhaps an hour he endeavored in vain to pick up a ship or a station in any of the South American countries. The signature he put to each message was "J. T." -- his own initials, but he could think of none better.

As he was about to give up his tests as a failure, he suddenly caught a faint clicking.

"J. T," came faintly to his ears.

He answered promptly.

"Who are you?" was the message he sent.

"U. S. cruiser Virginia," was the reply. "Who are you?"

"Survivors of merchant ship Albatross," Jack flashed back. "Castaways on uncharted island."

"What's your location?"

"Don't know. But there is a German submarine base on this island."

The wireless seemed nervous as the next message came in.

"What island?"

"Island called Kaiserland. There are also a nest of pirates here. We've just captured the wireless room."

"How long can you hold out?"

"Indefinitely."

"Good! I'll summon assistance and we'll search South American waters thoroughly. We'll find you sooner or later."

"Very well," Jack flashed back, "but be careful. These waters are infested with the enemy and they'll sink you if possble."

"Don't worry about us," was the Virginia's reply. "We can take care of ourselves. Can't you give me an idea where you are?"

Jack thought rapidly. Then he sent this:

"We were aboard a pirate ship three nights ago and sank a German raider 75 miles from this island. If you can pick up the wreck, we are due west."

"Thanks. We'll find it if it is still afloat. What's the strength of this pirate crew?"

"About fifty men."

"And the strength of the German submarine base, together with officers and men; also equipment?"

"Don't know," was Jack's reply. "I've only the pirate chief's word that there is a German submarine base. He is using a submarine stolen from the German as his own."

"Maybe he is lying to you," said the Virginia's wireless.

"Don't you believe it," Jack flashed back. "They're on this island all right."

"They won't be long, thanks to you," was the answer. "I'll pick you up later. I'm going to summon help."

The clicking of the wireless ceased. Jack waited impatiently for his call again, and at length it came.

"I've relayed your message to Washington," said the wireless. "I will have a fleet down here before long, but we'll come for you alone if necessary."

"Thanks," said Jack, "I --"

The lad broke off as Frank appeared in the door with a cry.

"Pirates coming back, Jack!" he cried. "Come on."

Jack delayed long enough to send this message:

"Pirates coming. Have to quit talking and fight. More later."

Before he removed the instrument from his head he caught this reply:

"Lick 'em good! Good luck."

Jack smiled to himself as he hurried from the wireless room and joined Frank and the others without.

"We may not lick 'em," he muttered, "but they'll know they've been in a fight."

Through the single window in the room Jack saw the returning pirates, Captain Jack in the lead, returning slowly.

"The good captain will be rather surprised when he finds his fortress has changed hands in his absence," said Jack to Frank.

"Rather," agreed Frank. "Now, what's the best plan? Step out and warn them away, or let them come close and do it then?"

"Let 'em come close," advised Jack. "There's only one window here to guard and we can do that without trouble. They don't have any artillery, so they can't batter down the door. Rifles won't do it. Let 'em come close and we'll give them a little scare."

Captain Jack led his pirate force toward the fort, unconscious of the danger that lay within. Captain Glenn and Williams had repaired the outer door so that it was now as strong as it had ever been.

Inside the stockade itself, Captain Jack approached the door wearily. He had had a hard and unsuccessful day and he was in no pleasant frame of mind. The door refused to budge when he pushed on it. Captain Jack raised his voice in a shout.

"I say there, Lawrence, what do you mean by locking me out? Open that door at once." For answer Jack opened the little window, and poking an automatic out before him, he said softly:

"Lawrence is a good pirate now, captain. We have him safely tied up."

Captain Jack stepped back in consternation. Then he reached for his gun.

"Hold on there!" shouted Jack. "I don't want to kill you, but I will if you make another move like that. Stand still now, like a real good pirate, and listen to what I have to say."

Captain Jack glared at Jack malevolently and for a moment it seemed that he might risk a shot for a chance to draw. Then his hands dropped to his side.

"All right," he said. "I'm listening."

"We're in command of this fort now," said Jack, "and we're going to stay in possession. You and the rest of your pirates will have to stay outside. Also you will have to rustle your own grub. We need all we have in here. Don't make the mistake of trying to catch us napping. We'll always be on guard, and you will find you are barking up the wrong tree. That's all. I'll give you five minutes to get out of range."

"So you've become pirates yourself, eh?" said Captain Jack, trying to keep his temper. "You steal our grub, and --"

"That's enough," said Jack, flourishing his revolver. "Your five minutes are growing short."

Captain Jack shook a threatening fist at Jack Templeton.

"I'll go!" he shouted, "but I'll come back and when I do you are going to be the sorriest Englishman I ever saw. You can lay to that. You can't make a fool of Captain Jack and live."

"I couldn't make a fool of you," said Jack. "That job was done before I ever saw you. Now go!"

A moment longer Captain Jack hesitated; then, as Jack raised his revolver, he turned and strode away.

The remainder of the pirates followed their chief.

CHAPTER XXV
CAPTURE OF CAPTAIN JACK

"He's telling the truth," said Jack, as he withdrew his head and shut the window. "He'll be back, all right, but I don't believe he'll try it tonight."

"Why?" asked Captain Glenn.

"Because he will figure that is what we expect him to do. No, I believe we will be secure enough here to-night."

"That's pretty good reasoning, Jack," said Frank. "But we'll be ready for the pirates when they do come."

"Nevertheless, it would be well to sleep with one eye open, so to speak," said Williams.

"Oh, we'll stand guard," said Jack. "We will not lay ourselves open to surprise by all going to bed at the same time. To my mind the night should be divided into three watches, as should the day. There are six of us. That means four hours' guard duty apiece."

"That's reasonable enough," Frank agreed. I'll take the first watch, if it's agreeable."

"Any way suits me," declared Captain Glenn.

"Then I'll pick you for second watch, Captain," said Jack. "I'll take the third. That will leave the day watch for Williams, Allen and Timothy."

Thus it was arranged. Frank began his watch at six o'clock that evening.

It was about an hour later when, as the others had gathered about them, Frank conceived a brilliant idea.

"By George!" he exclaimed suddenly.

"What's up?" asked Jack.

"Well," replied Frank, "I think I've got a plan that will save a lot of trouble."

"Let's hear it," said Williams.

"According to Jack's reasoning," said Frank, "we have little to fear from the pirates tonight."

"Right," said Jack. "What of it?"

"If your reasoning is good -- and I believe it is," Frank continued, "why can't we make a sortie tonight and capture the estimable Captain Jack? That would settle the whole business. Pirates without a leader would be like a ship without a rudder. What do you think about it?"

Jack considered the plan carefully before vouchsafing a reply. At length he said:

"Your plan, Frank, has all the earmarks of being successful. I believe you have solved the problem."

"So do I," declared Williams.

"I'm not so sure," said Captain Glenn. "Of course, no one will dispute that Frank's plan will solve the solution if it is successfully carried out. But there's the trouble. Should it fail, chances are some of us wouldn't be good for anything more. Besides, it would leave a harder task for those who survived."

"' Nothing risked, nothing gained," said Frank.

"That's true enough," said Captain Glenn, "but --"

"There is no use arguing," declared Jack. "Time grows short. Either we adopt the plan or we don't. We'll put it to vote. Frank, of course, votes for the plan and so do I. How about you, Williams?"

"Aye, sir," was the reply.

"Good! That's three. One more vote and it's decided. How about you, Timothy?"

"I vote yes," returned the sailor.

"That settles it, then," said Jack. "Captain Glenn, you're in the minority."

"All right," said the captain. "I'll make the vote unanimous if Allen is agreeable."

"Suits me, sir," was the reply.

"As it's my, plan," said Frank, "I ask to be allowed to lead the sortie. Some of us, of course, must stay here to protect the retreat of the others should they come back in a hurry."

"You're the doctor, Frank," said Jack.

"Very well. Then I elect to have you stay behind, Jack. Captain Glenn, Williams and I will do the work. You fellows who remain will be ready to admit us when we return."

"Trouble is," said Captain Glenn, "we don't know just where the pirates are encamped."

"I imagine we won't have much trouble finding out," said Frank.

"Then there is another thing," said Williams. "They may see us when we emerge from the stockade."

"I think not," said Frank. "First we will extinguish all lights. We can pass from the fort into the stockade, of course, without danger of being seen. Fortunately the night is dark. I am sure we can slip into the open unobserved."

"It's worth trying, at all events," declared Jack.

And so it was decided.

It was half past eleven o'clock by Jack's watch when Frank led the way from the fort. Behind him came Captain Glenn. Williams brought up the rear. Immediately they were outside, Jack closed and barred the door. Then he took up his silent vigil at the little window, prepared to unbar the door at a moment's notice should he see the others returning.

The three without flitted from the stockade like shadows. The night, as Frank had said, was very dark. Outside the stockade, the three threw themselves to the ground and crawled quietly toward the not far distant forest. They reached the shelter of the trees safely, then got to their feet.

Frank, acting upon impulse, led the way to the left, passing further into the forest as he advanced. After half an hour of careful walking, he stopped suddenly. The others halted at his side.

Frank pointed into the darkness. There, not ten yards away, Jay several sleeping figures. Frank knew they were members of the pirate band. The thing to do now was to single out the figure of Captain Jack.

Motioning the others to follow him, Frank stepped carefully in among the prostrate forms. He scanned each sleeper carefully, and at last he came upon a figure that he felt certain was the pirate captain.

This figure lay at full length, his face buried in one arm so Frank could not distinguish his features. But from the man's general build, the lad felt certain that he had picked the right man.

He motioned Captain Glenn and Williams to step close. Frank drew a previously prepared gag from his pocket and bent over the sleeper. Captain Glenn presented the muzzles of a pair of automatics squarely at the man, and Williams stooped over, armed with a length of rope. These precautions taken, Frank stirred the sleeper gently.

The man turned over and as he did so Frank clapped the gag to his mouth and tied it quickly. Then he lent a hand to Williams, and in spite of the gurgled protest of the victim, bound his hands. Frank then looked into the man's face.

He had picked aright. The man was Captain Jack.

The pirate, gazing into the weapons held by Captain Glenn, became suddenly quiet. Frank motioned him to proceed the way they had come. Captain Jack did so and stepped carefully over the sleeping men, as Frank, in a low voice, warned him to do.

Presently the three companions and their prisoner were beyond the circle of sleeping command.

"Now hurry," said Frank in a low voice.

At the same moment Captain Jack, in some manner, loosened the gag in his mouth and his voice rang out in a shout.

"Help! Help, men! Help!"

Frank realized the uselessness of further caution.

"Run!" he cried.

He whipped out his revolver, and as Captain Jack would have lingered, he fired at the ground. The bullet kicked up the shrubbery and the Captain, apparently believing the lad had attempted to shoot him, took to his heels with the others.

From behind came the sounds of confusion as the pirates, slumber-stricken, got to their feet, took in the situation and dashed to the chief's aid.

"Run your hardest!" cried Frank. "Don't hesitate or we shall be shot down as we cross the open."

But the moment gained as the pirates rubbed the sleep from their eyes sufficed.

Several times Frank urged Captain Jack to greater efforts by kicking up the dirt at his heels with a bullet from his revolver; but they entered the protection of the stockade at the same moment the first pirate reached the clearing that intervened and opened fire with his rifle.

As the four dashed across the stockade to the fort, Jack, who had not taken his eyes from the window since his friends left, quickly unbarred and threw open the door.

The four dashed inside. Quickly Jack barred the door again.

"Guns ready!" he cried. "The pirates may attack!"

Frank turned to Captain Jack.

"Well, my friend, Mr. Pirate Chief," he said with a grin, "we have you safe at last, eh?"

Captain Jack's only reply was a subdued growl.

CHAPTER XXVI
CONVERSION OF CAPTAIN JACK

"Here they come!" cried Jack from the window. Half a dozen forms flitted through the stockade gate and dashed toward the fort. Jack's revolver flashed twice and one man rolled over on the ground; but the others came on. Bullets struck close to the window as the pirates returned the fire.

"Here, Williams," said Frank, "take charge of Captain Jack. I'll lend Jack a hand at the window."

Regardless of the bullets that struck close, one every now and then coming through the window, Frank poked out his head and fired rapidly several times. Came howls of anguish and directly three men ran for the outer gate.

"Let 'em go," said Frank quietly. "Guess they won't bother us again for some time."

Jack slammed the window shut and dropped a heavy board down behind it. This was protection in case the pirates without tried their luck at shooting through the window.

"Give us some light, Captain Glenn," ordered Frank.

A moment later the interior of the fort was lighted up by the flare of half a dozen candles, Frank turned and surveyed the prisoner. .

"And how are you tonight, Captain Jack?" he asked.

The reply of the pirate chief was irrelevant.

"You've got me," he said, what do you think you are going to do with me?"

"We haven't figured that out yet," said Frank. "The first thing was to get you. We do one thing at a time, you see."

"Well, you've trouble on your hands now," said Captain Jack. "My men won't rest until they have released me."

"We'll risk that," said Frank. "Captain Glenn, I guess it is still you're watch. I'm going to lock our pirate up for the night and then I'm going to turn in."

"Same here," said Jack, and the others signified their agreement.

Frank conducted Captain Jack to the room where so recently he and his friends had been imprisoned. The key was in the door.

"Guess you'll sleep all right in here, Captain," said Frank.

He pushed his prisoner in the room and closed and locked the door behind him.

The night passed quietly. Allen 'rustled up breakfast the following morning and Frank conducted the pirate chief out to help eat it. Timothy stood guard at the window as the others ate.

"How'd you sleep, Captain?" asked Frank of the pirate chief.

"Not very well," was the reply.

"What's the matter, Captain? Conscience?"

"I was thinking, if that's what you mean," replied Captain Jack.

"I wouldn't be surprised if it were precisely what I mean," said Frank.

"Look here, Captain," said Jack, taking a hand in the conversation. "You're not half the bloodthirsty pirate you would have us believe. To tell the truth, I've taken quite a shine to you. In the right way, you could make a man of yourself."

"Thanks," said the pirate chief. "I've had those same thoughts, but I guess it's too late now."

"It's never too late," said Jack sententiously.

"Let me ask you a few questions."

"Fire away," said Captain Jack.

"All right. Now, you're an American, are you not?"

"Yes; a German-American, I guess you would call me."

"There is no longer such a thing as a German-American," Frank broke in. "Either you are an American, with the interests of the United States at heart, or you are a German and a subject of the Kaiser."

"Exactly," Jack agreed, "and for a man born and reared in America, as I judge you to have been, I cannot conceive how he could forsake the land of his birth for such brutes as the Germans have proved themselves to be in this war."

"My parents were German," said Captain Jack.

"That doesn't signify," said Jack. "America is their adopted country and I am sure that you would find them standing by Uncle Sam."

"You are probably right," admitted Captain Jack. I can recall tales my father told of the downtrodden people of his native land. Today he is probably standing by America to the best of his ability. Truth is, though, I haven't paid much attention the rights and wrongs of this war, My sympathies, naturally enough, were with Germany before the United States was drawn into the conflict. That, of course, was because of my German ancestry. Since the United States entered the war I have been an enemy to both sides. I have robbed Germany and the United States alike, and still, so far, I have killed no man."

"But can't you see," said Frank, "that your present life can result in no good and that, on the other hand, there is much you can do for your country?"

"Oh, I can see it, all right," was Captain Jack's reply. "I'll tell you something. I really hadn't thought much about it until I encountered you fellows. You two," indicating Frank and Jack, "are both young and brave and have done some things to be proud of. Here I am, older than either of you, and I'm just a pirate. Since I first ran across you I have thought considerably of the things that might have been, but it's too late now."

"I tell you it is never too late," said Jack. "There is still time for you to mend your ways and do something for your country. You are a brave man and there is little that a brave man cannot accomplish if he only tries. Just say the word and we will all be willing to lend you a helping you."

Captain Jack got to his feet, amazement written on his countenance.

"You mean that?" he cried.

"Of course," said Jack.

Frank nodded.

"We'll do what we can," he said.

"But I'm a law-breaker," said Captain Jack. "I should be punished."

"I agree with you there," said Frank. "I would not raise a hand to lighten your punishment, for I feel you deserve it. But every man must pay for his own misdeeds. The thing for you to do now is to expiate, so far as possible, your past crimes by turning yourself to doing what is right and good."

"By George!" exclaimed Captain Jack, and brought his great fist down on the table with a resounding crash, "you are right. Just tell me what to do and I'll do it."

Jack smiled.

"A man should have to work out his own plan of redemption," he said, "and yet I believe I can help you."

"How?" demanded Captain Jack eagerly.

"I'll explain," said Jack. The others listened anxiously. "You have told us," Jack continued, "that there is a German submarine base on this island. You were telling the truth?"

"I was," said Captain Jack. "I stole my submarine, the Roger, from the Germans on the island."

"All right. Now you could do your native land -- America -- an invaluable service by destroying that base."

Frank and the others started to their feet at this. It was the first inkling they had had of a plan that had long been fomenting in Jack's mind.

"By George, Jack! A bully idea!" cried Frank. "Why didn't you mention it before?"

"Because we were in no position to carry it out," was Jack's reply.

Captain Jack's face grew red. His eyes flashed.

"A good idea," he said quietly to Jack. "I have no doubt it can be accomplished, though it will of course be dangerous."

"And you are willing to undertake it?" asked Frank, surprised.

"Of course. But I would be alone for a while, that I may think. Have you any objections to my retiring to the next room? I give you my word I shall not attempt to escape."

Jack took the words out of Frank's mouth.

"Go ahead," he said.

Captain Glenn was the first to speak after Captain Jack had left the room.

"Don't you think this conversion is rather sudden?" he asked. "Is the estimable Captain Jack not taking this means to throw us off our guard?"

"I don't think so," replied Jack quietly. "I have studied the man carefully since I have known him and I have discovered that, try as he will, he is not pleased with the life of a pirate. I can see, too, that be craves action, and it may have been only natural, for that reason, that he turned to piracy. I am willing to take his word that he will do what he says whenever he is willing to give it."

"And so am I!" declared Frank.

"It looks pretty fishy to me," declared Captain Glenn, but Williams sided with the two lads.

Half an hour later Captain Jack returned. Walking up to the table he extended a hand each to Jack and Frank.

"You can count on me," he said simply, and added with a half smile, "if you are not afraid to trust an erstwhile pirate."

Frank and Jack grasped the extended hands and gripped them warmly.

"Not a bit of it," they said in a single voice, and Frank added: "We are glad to have a man like you with us."

And thus came about the conversion of Captain Jack, pirate.

CHAPTER XXVII
CAPTAIN JACK'S MEN REBEL

"There are only seven of us here," said Frank, a short time later. "Strikes me we won't have a whole lot of success raiding the German submarine base."

"Don't forget my fifty pirates," said Captain Jack.

"Great Scott!" ejaculated Captain Glenn. "I hope you don't want me to think that crowd of pirates will listen to you when they hear you have reformed."

"Don't you worry about my pirates," said Captain Jack with a smile. "Just leave them to me. Most of them are either English, French, Americans or Italians. There are a couple of negroes and some Brazilians and Chileans. I'll probably have trouble with the South Americans, but I feel sure the others will join me in whatever I ask."

"I wouldn't be too sure about that," said Captain Glenn.

"I thought most of your men were South Americans," said Frank. "That's the way they impressed me."

"You must remember you haven't seen the most of them," said Captain Jack. "But come, we may as well have the job over with. Will you accompany me?"

"We will," said Captain Glenn decisively.

Captain Jack turned on him.

"You don't trust me," he said.

"You're right," said Captain Glenn briefly. "I don't."

Captain Jack's fists clenched. He was about to make an angry retort, but Frank forestalled him.

"You can't blame him, Captain Jack," the lad said. "It's only an hour ago that you were a pirate of the first water, you know."

Captain Jack's fingers straightened out again.

"That's true," he muttered.

He led the way from the fort and out of the stockade into the clearing beyond.

Shouts from the distance told Frank and Jack that the pirates had seen the approach of their chief, and they hailed him with glad cries.

"They seem to think a lot of him," said Jack to Frank.

"Why shouldn't they?" was Frank's reply. "He's done a lot for them, from their viewpoint. Also, it's plain to be seen that they have a wholesome respect for him. I haven't told you how handy he is with a gun."

"That so?" said Jack. "Guess I'd bet on you in a pinch, though."

"You'd probably lose," said Frank dryly, and explained the result of his first encounter with Captain Jack.

"Whew!" said Jack. "No wonder his men respect him."

The pirates now came forth from among the trees to greet their chief. Their expressions indicated that they were clearly surprised at Captain Jack's apparent friendliness with the foe, but no man ventured a word.

Captain Jack motioned them to gather around. Frank, Jack and the others a moment later found themselves in the center of the ring of pirates. Captain Glenn's hands, in his pockets, grasped his revolvers firmly. The American sea captain was determined not to be caught off his guard. He was perfectly certain in his own mind that Captain Jack was bent on mischief.

As the pirates drew closer, Frank and Jack also dropped their hands to their automatics. In his heart each lad trusted Captain Jack, but each had decided in his own mind that it was better to be prepared.

"Men," said Captain Jack, addressing the rabble, "as I lay a prisoner in the fort during the night, it came to me that we are all wasting our lives in our present manner of living. Sooner or later we are sure to be captured and hanged. I've thought it all out and I've come to the conclusion that the life of a pirate is no life for me -- nor for any of the rest of you. Therefore, I have decided to be a pirate no longer."

Shouts of surprise -- and anger came from the assembled men. Amazement was written large upon every face. The man called Jackson, the same who had locked up the lads and their friends when they first entered the fort, stepped forward.

"You mean that you are going to desert us?" he asked.

Captain Jack shook his head.

"Not at all," he replied quietly. "I mean that I am going to call upon you to join me in a new adventure, but one that is within the law."

There were wild hurrahs from the men. Jackson's face turned dark as he turned upon them.

"Wait until you know what this new venture is, men," he cried.

Frank and Jack exchanged significant gestures. It was plain to them that this man Jackson had no love for Captain Jack and that he had only been biding his time to turn the pirates against their leader.

Captain Jack smiled.

"I'll tell them, Jackson, have no fear," he said. He turned again and addressed the men.

"What I want you to do, men," he said, "is to become true citizens of the world and join me in striking a blow at the German submarine base on the island. The Germans are the enemies of all mankind. They must be destroyed. Will you help me give the island of Kaiserland a new name?"

For several moments there was a dead silence as the men digested their leader's words. The silence was broken by Jackson. Springing quickly forward, he threw up his right hand and shouted:

"Listen to me, men. Captain Jack here, most likely, has been promised immunity for his crimes by these new friends of his. He's trying to lead you on to death or the gallows. I, for one, refuse longer to recognize his leadership. Who is with me?"

But the men, apparently, were not yet ready to take sides. Captain Jack smiled at Jackson; then his face grew stern.

"I'll attend to you directly, Jackson," he said quietly. "Now, men, you know me well enough to know I am not trying to betray you. I am asking you, for once, to do a good deed. Most of you are Americans, French, Italian or British. Your countries are at war with Germany. Will you not strike a blow when you have the chance? It is true, there will be no rich booty for us, nothing but danger and perhaps death, but there will be riches greater than booty after all; for the adventure that I propose will bring to each man the consciousness of a duty well done, and that is more than gold. Men, we have been together for many months. I have not failed you in the past. Will you fail me now?"

There were wild cries of "No! No!" and "Destruction to the Germans," but there also were voices raised in protest.

Jackson, realizing that his chances were fast slipping away, determined upon a bold stroke. With a sudden cry he sprang toward Captain Jack, a knife gleaming in his hand.

Frank uttered a cry of warning and his revolver flashed out.

Captain Jack saw the lad's movement from the comer of his eye, and before the lad could press the trigger, he cried sharply:

"Don't shoot! Leave this man to me."

He avoided Jackson's rush by a quick side step, and as lie prepared to defend himself, he explained to Frank:

"One shot might prove our undoing. It would set the men wild. I can handle this fellow. Don't interfere, or allow any of the others to do so, no matter what happens."

Frank returned his revolver to his pocket.

Jackson, who had been carried beyond Captain Jack by the impetus of his spring when Captain Jack stepped aside, now wheeled about and returned to the attack, his gleaming knife rised above his head. Captain Jack, with no weapon in his hand, although he wore both revolver and knife in his belt, waited for him calmly. His arms were spread wide apart and both feet were implanted firmly in the ground. He smiled slightly.

Apparently he presented an uninviting aspect, for Jackson hesitated in his rush. This hesitancy caused his undoing.

Captain Jack leaped forward with a mighty spring. His strong right arm encircled Jackson's neck, while his left hand clutched Jackson's knife arm. Jackson was borne over backwards and Captain Jack went down on top of him.

There was a sharp snap and the knife that Jackson held went flying through the air. Captain Jack's powerful fingers had broken the man's wrist. At the same moment Captain Jack drove his right fist into Jackson's face. Then he got to his feet and faced the others.

"Any more of you want my job?" he cried, his face red with anger.

No man stepped forth.

"I thought not," said Captain Jack. "Very well. Now, you have heard my proposition. You are free to accept or refuse it at your pleasure. As for me, I am going through with it, anyhow. Which of you are with me?"

Came cries of "I am, Captain! I am," and the men rushed forward.

Captain Jack smiled again. He was his old self now. He turned to Frank and Jack.

"You see," he said quietly, "I was sure of my men."

"Well, you know how to handle them, that's certain," said Jack admiringly. "Tell them to follow us back to the fort. Then we'll lay our plans."

Captain Jack gave the necessary command. Frank led the way back. The men followed, talking excitedly among themselves, all save Jackson, who was carried by two of his comrades.

CHAPTER XXVIII
PLANNING THE ATTACK

"Think I'll have a little confab with my friend Virginia," said Jack, soon after they had returned to the fort.

"With whom?" asked Captain Jack.

"Oh, we haven't told you about that, have we?" said Jack. "I mean the United States cruiser Virginia. I picked her up on the wireless yesterday."

"You did, eh?" laughed Captain Jack. "Did you give them our location?"

"I didn't know it," said Jack.

"Well," said Captain Jack, "if you'll let me do the talking this time I'll give it to them."

"Better give them the location of the submarine base, instead," said Jack. "We'll make our start tonight, and it might be well to have a cruiser or two drop in at the finish. But I didn't know you were a wireless operator."

"I'm not much of one," returned Captain Jack, "but I'm not so bad, either."

The two went into the wireless room, where Captain Jack adjusted the receiver over his head. Then he began to flash the Virginia call into space; and at last he got an answer.

"Kaiserland?" came the query.

"Yes," Captain Jack flashed back.

"Who's sending?"

Captain Jack hesitated a moment and then replied:

"Pirate chief."

"So you have captured the other party, eh?"

"No, we've just joined forces. We are going to raid the German submarine base tonight."

"Are you telling the truth or trying to throw me off the trail?"

"I'm telling the truth. The man you talked to yesterday is here, if you care to talk to him."

"Let me talk to him."

Jack took Captain Jack's place at the wireless. It took some conversation to convince the commander of the Virginia that all was well but Jack did it at last and gave the location Captain Jack gave him,

"We haven't been able to pick up any wreck," said the Virginia, "and we had about given up hope of finding you. We tried all night and all morning to pick you up."

"We were busy," said Jack.

"You must have been," was the answer. "You say you will make the raid to-night?"

"Yes; when can you get on the ground?"

"Not before morning. Maybe you had better wait so we can join forces."

"Not much," Jack flashed back. "This is my, plan and I'm going to do the work."

"All right, but be careful. I'll put other vessels in this water in touch and have them on the scene as soon as possible."

"All right," said Jack. "How many vessels in these waters?"

"Half a dozen."

"Well, you'd better get as many of them as possible on the scene," said Jack. "There might be a slip, you know."

"I'll do the best I can. Good-by and good luck to you."

"Good-by!" flashed Jack.

"Not much help to be expected from that source, unless we wait," the lad said to Captain Jack.

"Well, we don't want to wait," said the chief of the pirates.

"Right you are as you are."

"I'm just as anxious for action."

They returned to the other room, where Jack called a council of war.

"The time to strike is now," he said when the others had gathered around the table, all except the pirates, who were still outside.

"I agree with you," said Frank. "How long a march is it, Captain Jack?"

"If we leave here two hours before dark we will reach the base soon after midnight," was the reply; "but if you will allow me, I have a plan to suggest."

"Let's hear it, Captain," said Jack.

"To my way of thinking," said Captain Jack, "it would be better if we attack from two places."

"Two places?" echoed Frank.

"Yes. My plan would be to send the bulk of the men afoot, while I pick a crew for my submarine and strike from the sea."

"By Jove!" said Jack. "A first class idea! But will not the German submarine base be mined?"

"It wasn't when I was there before," said Captain Jack significantly. "Otherwise I would not have come out whole with a submarine."

"That's true," said Jack. "Well, I agree with you. Yours is by far the best plan. How many men do you need aboard the submarine?"

"Not more than fifteen. The others will go a foot."

"There is a hitch in this plan, though," said Frank.

"What is it?' demanded Captain Jack.

"Well, your men may be willing to follow you all right, but will they follow me, or Jack here? You can't go by land and by sea both, you know, Captain."

"By George!" exclaimed Captain Jack. "I hadn't thought of that. However, I have no doubt it can be remedied."

"I think I can point out the remedy," said Captain Glenn.

"What is it, Captain?"

"Well, Frank and Jack here know something about submarines, they tell me. My advice would be to put one of them in command of your men aboard the submarine rather than in command of the land party. Chances are none of your men know aught of navigation and would have to depend upon the man in command, whereas, on land, they might think they could shift for themselves."

"I am of your opinion, Captain," said Captain Jack, "and shall act upon your advice. Now, is Templeton or Chadwick the better man for the job?"

"I fancy one will do as well as the other," put in Williams.

"Personally," said Frank, "I should like the job myself."

"It's yours, then," said Captain Jack briefly.

"Maybe the men will object," said Frank.

"Let 'em," returned Captain Jack. "I'll fix that."

"That's arranged then," said Jack. "Next thing, Captain Jack, is to select the men for the crew. Williams, you'd better go aboard the submarine as first officer."

"Suits me," said Williams briefly.

"I'll draw up a list of the crew," said Captain Jack.

He produced an old envelope and a lead pencil and scribbled. Directly he pushed back his chair.

"That's done," he said. "What next?"

"What's the lay of the land, Captain?" asked Jack.

"Well," replied the pirate chief, "I'll give Chadwick here a chart that he will find sufficient for his purposes. I made it, thinking I might want a second submarine some day."

"But how about the land party?" asked Jack.

"The German base," said Captain Jack, "extends along the southern extremity of the island for perhaps a mile. You see, therefore, that it's small. I don't believe there are more than a dozen submarines there. Whether there are more large raiders, I can't say. I wouldn't be surprised, however, if the one you put a torpedo into the other night was the last. That would mean that ashore, besides whatever number of the submarine crews that are aboard their vessels, there would be comparatively few men. We'll count the submarine crews as twenty-five men to a ship. That's 300 men. There may be an additional hundred men on the ground, but I doubt it."

"But they must have some means of protection," said Jack. "Big guns, and rifles a-plenty."

"Rifles, yes," was the reply, "but few big guns. They feel so secure in their hiding places that they have made use of their guns mostly to arm merchant raiders."

"I see," said Jack. "Well, we'll have to leave something to chance. Now the question arises as how best to destroy the place, submarines and all."

"Well, I can fix that, too," said Captain Jack. "Bombs are the things to do the trick. Half a dozen bombs scattered about and timed nicely, and there won't be a German submarine base at this time tomorrow."

"All right so far as the land side goes," said Frank, "but how about the submarines?"

"Mines," said Captain Jack quietly, "timed to explode simultaneously with the bombs ashore. You can lay them from the submarine."

"By Jove!" said Jack. "You'd make a first class combined general-admiral, Captain Jack," declared Captain Glenn.

Captain Jack smiled slowly.

"I've had all this planned for many a day," he said quietly. "I didn't know when the Germans might declare war on me, and when they did I was determined to exterminate them."

"Well, plans thus being decided upon," said Frank, "there is nothing to do but await the hour of departure."

They discussed the plans in detail while they waited, however. At four o'clock Captain Jack got to his feet.

"Time to get busy," he said.

CHAPTER XXIX
IN THE NIGHT

Frank took command of the submarine. As he had feared, there was some protest among the men Captain Jack had decided upon to man the vessel, but the pirate chief soon overcame this. Therefore, when the submarine put off from Kaiserland, the men were anxious to obey the lad's every order.

From the fort to the place where the submarine lay the paths of both land and sea parties lay together. According to Captain Jack's calculations the start from this point, if made simultaneously by land and sea forces, would enable both to reach their destination at approximately the same hour, if the submarine was held to five knots an hour. It had been deemed advisable for the undersea craft to go some distance from land and then run south submerged.

From the deck of the submarine Frank waved a band to his friends on shore. The others stood watching while the vessel crept through the water. At length, upon Frank's order, it submerged.

Captain Jack ordered his men south.

The land party now was divided into three sections. Captain Jack led the main body, composed of twelve men. Jack had the same number under his command. Counting Timothy and Allen, Captain Glenn commanded thirteen men.

While Jack was nominally in command of the party, it had been decided that it would be wise to let Captain Jack show the way, this because the pirates would feel more secure under his guidance. They moved south at a rapid walk.

Darkness fell and still the marchers made their way through the thick trees and underbrush. The march would be a long one, so after two hours' walking, Captain Jack slowed his men down a trifle.

At 10 o'clock Captain Jack called a halt in the darkness. He glanced at his watch by the dim light of the moon, and passed the word for Jack and Captain Glenn, who approached a moment later.

"Half an hour's march and we shall be within sight of the base," said Captain Jack. "The Germans have felled trees between them and the forest proper, apparently with the idea of preventing a surprise from this direction. We'll have to trust to luck and the darkness to get us safely across opening."

"We'll take it at a run," said Captain Glenn.

"That will be the best way," Captain Jack agreed, but I figure we had better approach from different points. Templeton, I'll wait here with my men while you make a quarter of a mile detour to the right. Captain Glenn, you do the same to the left. I'll wait here fifteen minutes. When you see the first of my men move across the opening, you follow suit."

"A good idea," was Jack's comment.

"Don't forget," Captain Jack said, "that the main thing is to get the bombs planted without being discovered. If we can do that without interruption, it would even be well to draw off without firing a shot. But the bombs must be placed squarely within the German settlement or our work will count for nothing."

"Right you are, Captain," said Captain Glenn.

"Very good, then. Now, you fellows get to your places and then move toward the clearing. As soon as you see my men moving across the opening, advance."

Jack and Captain Glenn returned to their commands and gave the necessary marching orders.   The men moved off in the darkness.

Less than an hour later Jack stood in the shelter of a large tree at the very edge of the clearing. In the distance he could make out what appeared to be numerous buildings. This was the point, the lad felt sure, where the blow would be struck.

In his left hand Jack carried a small but powerful bomb, which had been provided by Captain Jack. The fuse attached would burn fifteen minutes. In the time after it was lighted this meant that the attacking party had fifteen minutes to get out of the way before the explosion occurred. Captain Glenn and Captain Jack carried similar explosives.

Jack kept his eyes upon the place where Captain, Jack's party soon was to move across the open. For five minutes he gazed without result, and then he saw several shadowy figures stealing across the clearing.

Jack turned to his men with a command.

"March!" he ordered.

He placed himself at their head and they dashed through the darkness at a run.

A quarter of a mile on the other side of Captain Jack's party, Captain Glenn also had ordered his men forward.

Meanwhile, what of Frank and the submarine?

Shaping his course by the chart which Captain Jack had given him, Frank kept the course accurately. The speed of the vessel was maintained at five knots, in accordance with Captain Jack's calculations. As Frank's watch showed half past eleven, he felt that the time to exercise the greatest caution had come.

The lad turned the wheel over to Williams and took the latter's place at the periscope. Directly he was able to make out the coast line, and even at this distance he felt certain that he could make out a long row of buildings in the background. The submarine was, of course, still too far away for possible vessels, which would lie low on the water, to be within the lad's range of vision.

"Where are the mines?" the lad asked Williams.

"Foot of the ladder, sir," was the reply.

"Fuses attached?"

"Yes, sir, and anchors, too, sir."

"Good! Of course, we'll have to come to the surface to let them go."

"Of course, sir."

'Then be ready when I give the word. I can't pick up any submarines at this distance, but they may all be upon the surface as well as resting beneath the water."

"I'm ready, sir."

"Torpedoes all right?"

"Yes, sir. I just examined them ten minutes ago."

"Guess there are no other precautions we can take," said Frank. "Be ready to grab a couplr of mines and follow me on deck when I give the word." Frank turned and summoned one of the pirate crew, a negro, who answered to the name of Jefferson.

"Jefferson, take the wheel," he said.

Jefferson did so, grinning.

"Slow to two knots, Williams," ordered Frank.

Williams signaled the engine room and the pace of the submarine slowed down until the vessel was barely moving through the water.

Frank glanced at his watch. It was 12 o'clock.

"Fifteen minutes in which to lay the mines," he said to himself. "They must explode at 12:30 --"

At 12:10 the submarine emerged from the depth and floated calmly upon the surface of what appeared to be an artificial harbor. Frank and Williams, leaving Jefferson at the wheel and ordering the engines stopped, sprang on deck, carrying two small packages each. These, bound in little tin boxes, were the deadly mines.

"One off herc, Williams," said Frank, putting one on deck and glancing at his watch.

The hands showed 12:15.

"We'll have to work fast," said Frank.

Quickly Frank dropped one of the mines over the port side of the vessel, aft. Williams followed suit to starboard, forward. Frank poked his head down the hatchway and yelled:

"Full speed, ahead, Jefferson!" The vessel dashed forward. "West by north five points!" yelled Frank.

The submarine veered sharply.

Two minutes from where the first mines had been dropped overboard, Frank and Williams let go the remaining two. As they did so, Frank perceived several long shapes emerging from below. He took one look and then dived below with a cry to Williams:

"Submarines!"

It was true. Attracted by the impending danger in some unaccountable fashion, the German terrors of the deep were coming from fancied security beneath the waves for a look around.

Frank grabbed the wheel from Jefferson and turned the head of the submarine due north. He rang for full speed ahead.

At almost the same instant one of the German submarines espied the stranger in the midst. There was a hail across the water. Then a torpedo flashed close to the Roger.

Again Frank glanced at his watch. It was 12:25 -- only five minutes were left in which the pirate submarine might reach a place of safety. Frank feared to give the signal to submerge for the reason that the speed of the craft would be impeded.

It was better to run the gauntlet of the submarines on top of the water. Torpedoes passed close, but Frank maneuvered the little vessel from port to starboard and back again so rapidly that none struck home.

And at last Frank, watch in hand, felt that the submarine was safely out of the danger zone. His watch showed 12:30.

Frank strained his ears to catch the explosion that would tell him the deadly mines had done their work.

CHAPTER XXX
CAPTAIN JACK PAYS

The attacking party, led by Jack Templeton, Captain Jack and Captain Glenn, advanced across the clearing toward the unsuspecting German settlement at a run.

The distance was perhaps two hundred yards and Captain Jack felt that if this distance could be transversed without discovery, the success of the raid was assured.

But the distance was not to be covered without discovery.

Half way across the open a shot rang out. This was quickly followed by three more. One of the men under Captain Glenn's command pitched forward on his face.

"Forward, men!" cried Captain Glenn, springing forward faster than before.

Captain Jack and Jack Templeton also urged their men to redoubled efforts.

Within the German lines, Jack saw men running forward. Apparently the German officers were trying to get their men in formation to ward off an attack. The enemy had no means of ascertaining the strength of the attacking party, attack was ordered.

Although Frank did not know it, it was the sounds of the firing on shore that had brought the German submarines in the harbor from the depths, upon command, to lend a helping hand if need be.

A volley broke from the three divisions of raiders as they dashed for the German lines. Now that their presence had been discovered there was no reason for further efforts at concealment, and Captain Jack and the other leaders had no mind to be fired upon without returning the compliment.

The result of the volleys, the raiders had no means of determining, but they felt sure that some of the bullets had found human marks. Time after time the Germans fired at the advancing' men, but as the latter showed no signs of giving up the attack the German commander ordered his men to fall back toward the water's edge. He naturally supposed that, his base having been discovered, he was being attacked in force. He could have no idea that the raid was being conducted by a small body of desperate men.

The plan of the German commander was to make a stand at the water edge and then rush his men aboard the flotilla of submarines should he be pressed too closely.

This decision was fortunate for the raiders, for had the Germans made a determined stand the attack must have failed.

Captain Jack's party was the first to reach the settlement. Volley after volley they poured into the Germans. Jack and his men arrived next, and soon Captain Glenn's command, bearing down from the flank, reinforced the first arrivals.

Captain Jack hurled his bomb as far forward as possible at precisely 12:15. From their sections of the field Jack and Captain Glenn followed suit at the same time. Then each commander ordered a retreat.

As the raiders turned and ran, the German commander's first thought was to order a pursuit. But he changed his mind quickly, for he feared the retreat might be only a ruse to draw him on. For that reason he ordered his men to stay, for the moment, where they were.

As members of the raiding party dashed back over the ground they had traversed, however, the German rifles poured volleys after them. Captain Jack was bringing up the rear of his party. So it was that no man saw him suddenly pitch forward on his face. Captain Jack drew himself slowly to his feet and as slowly retreated again. There was a terrible pain in his left side and he realized that a German bullet, entering his back, had gone clear through him. Blood flowed profusely and the pirate chief knew that he was badly wounded. Nevertheless, he did not call after his men, but followed them as swiftly as he could.

Now the German commander decided that the retreat of the foe was not a ruse to draw him on. He ordered his men forward and volley after volley was fired over Captain Jack's head at the retreating pirates.

At the edge of the forest beyond, the pirates turned, and then, for the first time, they realized that Captain Jack had been left behind. Wild yells shattered the stillness of the night. In the face of almost certain death, the pirates wheeled and dashed to the rescue of their chief.

But the Germans also were dashing forward. As Captain Jack saw his men rushing back to him, and realized the fate that threatened them, he waved them away, shouting:

"Go back! I'll make it, all right."

Then, as the pirates disregarded this and still came on, he ordered them again to fall back.

"Don't forget the bombs!" he cried.

There are few men who will advance into the face of certain death. These pirates were not of these few. A quarter of a mile away to either side, it was impossible for Jack or Captain Glenn or their men to render assistance; and now the other pirates turned again and took to their heels.

So Captain Jack was left alone to face the oncoming Germans.

First Captain Jack took time to glance at his watch. The hands pointed to 12:25.

"I would like to live five minutes yet," he muttered.

He discarded his now empty rifle and produced his pair of automatics.

The Germans, seeing but one man opposing their path, rushed forward to make him a prisoner.

"Crack! Crack! Crack! Crack!"

Both of Captain Jack's revolvers were flashing fire.

"Crack! Crack! Crack! Crack!" they spoke again.

And so until each weapon had been emptied of ten shots. Captain Jack hurled his useless weapons in the very faces of his foes and again produced his watch.

The hands showed 12:30.

"Time!" said Captain Jack, and at that moment a German bullet laid him low.

But Captain Jack was not dead. He raised his head and listened; and then what he waited for came.

There was a terrible rumble and roar, followed by two ear-splitting blasts. These were quickly succeeded by others. The ground rocked and swayed. Men, huge wooden buildings, steel and iron within the German lines went sailing high in the air, to come down for miles around.

Terrible screams and groans and curses shattered the night, quickly followed by more detonations somewhat muffled, as the mines dropped from the pirate submarine exploded beneath the water.

The waves were lashed into a frenzy. The ground trembled for long minutes and seemed on the point of dropping into the bowels of the earth.

And then it began to rain men and debris.

Great rocks, brought up from deep in the earth, fell on all sides of the place where Captain Jack lay wounded unto death, but as though by a miracle none touched him. Where the pirates were still racing for safety, with Jack and Captain Glenn at their head, trees were uprooted and toppled over. The rain of steel and iron and rocks carried even there, and the men threw themselves to the ground and put their arms above their heads.

And then, as suddenly as it had begun, the rain of missiles ceased.

Jack got to his feet, as did his men. Rapidly he led them back toward where a moment before had been a German submarine base.

There was no base there now. Nothing but ruin and destruction and death. The German submarine base, submarines in the harbor, men who had inhabited the place, had passed into oblivion.

The raid had been complete.

Captain Glenn also returned to the front with his men, and the pirates who had been under Captain Jack's command, dashed back to search for their captain.

The sea had now become calm again and Frank ordered the submarine headed for the harbor. Half an hour later he went ashore, accompanied by Williams and every member of the crew.

Frank was appalled at the extent of the destruction. Rapidly he passed through the ruins toward the forest beyond, where he knew he would find Jack or some trace of him. And there he came upon the sad band of pirates.

Into the midst of these Frank forced his way. In the center, his head on Jack's knee, was Captain Jack. Blood flowed from wounds in the back of his head, from his forehead and from his sides. He was unconscious.

But as Frank bent down beside him, the pirate chief opened his eyes. He saw Jack and Frank and smiled his old smile.

"Was the raid a success?" he asked feebly.

"It was," replied Jack quietly. "Not a German left alive, nor one stone upon another nor a submarine in the harbor."

"Good!" said the pirate chief. "I would like to speak to my men."

At a signal from Jack these gathered around him.

"Men," said Captain Jack, "I am going to a land where there is no piracy and no wars. But before I go I want to tell you that I repented of my evil ways before it was too late; and I want the promise of each one of you that from this time on he will lead an upright life -- a peaceful life at such time that his services are not being employed in the service of his native land. I want to shake hands with each one of you and hear your promise."

Sadly the men filed by him and there was none who did not promise freely all that the pirate chief asked. Then they stood near with downcast heads.

Captain Jack shook hands with Williams and Captain Glenn.

"You see I was to be trusted, after all," he said.

Captain Glenn pressed the hand but made no reply.

From the distance there came a dull rumble. Frank stood up and gazed toward the harbor through the darkness. Suddenly a powerful glare lighted up the shore.

"What is that?" demanded Captain Jack, freeing himself from Jack and getting to his feet in spite of his wounds.

"Searchlight," replied Frank briefly. "Probably the Varginia approaching to give us aid."

"We don't need it now," said Captain Jack.

He extended a hand to Jack and one to Frank and the lads pressed them warmly. As they stood thus, Captain Jack's body swayed slightly and became limp. Gently the boys laid him on the ground. They bent over to catch the sound of his voice.

"Tell America that I have been of some good after all," said Captain Jack, pirate chief, in a low voice.

And so he died.

From across the sea came the sound of a big gun. Swiftly toward the island of Kaiserland came the American cruiser Virginia.

Here, beside the body of the dead pirate chief on an uncharted island in the South Atlantic, ends our story. Subsequent adventures of Frank Chadwick and Jack Templeton will be related in a succeeding volume, entitled "The Boy Allies with the Submarine D-32; or, The Fall of the Russian Empire."

THE END

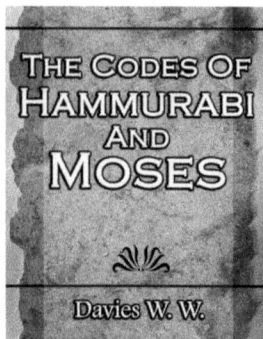

The Codes Of Hammurabi And Moses
W. W. Davies

QTY

The discovery of the Hammurabi Code is one of the greatest achievements of archaeology, and is of paramount interest, not only to the student of the Bible, but also to all those interested in ancient history...

Religion   ISBN: *1-59462-338-4*   Pages:132

MSRP $12.95

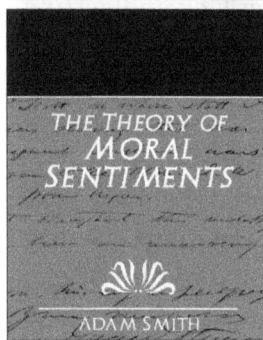

The Theory of Moral Sentiments
Adam Smith

QTY

This work from 1749. contains original theories of conscience amd moral judgment and it is the foundation for systemof morals.

Philosophy ISBN: *1-59462-777-0*   Pages:536

MSRP $19.95

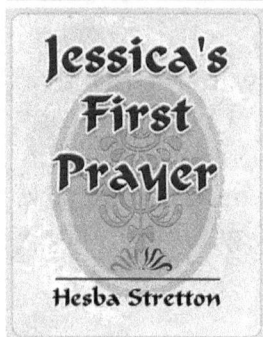

Jessica's First Prayer
Hesba Stretton

QTY

In a screened and secluded corner of one of the many railway-bridges which span the streets of London there could be seen a few years ago, from five o'clock every morning until half past eight, a tidily set-out coffee-stall, consisting of a trestle and board, upon which stood two large tin cans, with a small fire of charcoal burning under each so as to keep the coffee boiling during the early hours of the morning when the work-people were thronging into the city on their way to their daily toil...

Pages:84

Childrens   ISBN: *1-59462-373-2*   *MSRP $9.95*

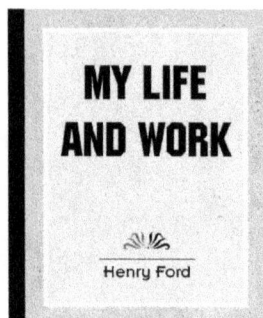

My Life and Work
Henry Ford

QTY

Henry Ford revolutionized the world with his implementation of mass production for the Model T automobile. Gain valuable business insight into his life and work with his own auto-biography... "We have only started on our development of our country we have not as yet, with all our talk of wonderful progress, done more than scratch the surface. The progress has been wonderful enough but..."

Pages:300

Biographies/   ISBN: *1-59462-198-5*   *MSRP $21.95*

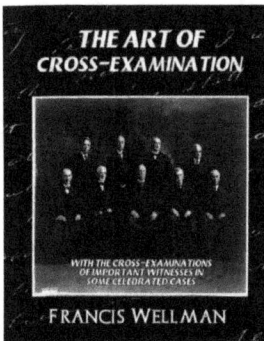

The Art of Cross-Examination
Francis Wellman

QTY

I presume it is the experience of every author, after his first book is published upon an important subject, to be almost overwhelmed with a wealth of ideas and illustrations which could readily have been included in his book, and which to his own mind, at least, seem to make a second edition inevitable. Such certainly was the case with me; and when the first edition had reached its sixth impression in five months, I rejoiced to learn that it seemed to my publishers that the book had met with a sufficiently favorable reception to justify a second and considerably enlarged edition. ..

Pages:412

Reference   ISBN: *1-59462-647-2*   *MSRP $19.95*

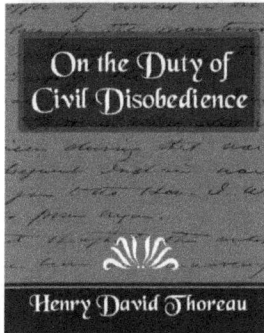

On the Duty of Civil Disobedience
Henry David Thoreau

QTY

Thoreau wrote his famous essay, On the Duty of Civil Disobedience, as a protest against an unjust but popular war and the immoral but popular institution of slave-owning. He did more than write—he declined to pay his taxes, and was hauled off to gaol in consequence. Who can say how much this refusal of his hastened the end of the war and of slavery ?

Law   ISBN: *1-59462-747-9*   **Pages:48**

MSRP $7.45

Dream Psychology Psychoanalysis for Beginners
Sigmund Freud

QTY

Sigmund Freud, born Sigismund Schlomo Freud (May 6, 1856 - September 23, 1939), was a Jewish-Austrian neurologist and psychiatrist who co-founded the psychoanalytic school of psychology. Freud is best known for his theories of the unconscious mind, especially involving the mechanism of repression; his redefinition of sexual desire as mobile and directed towards a wide variety of objects; and his therapeutic techniques, especially his understanding of transference in the therapeutic relationship and the presumed value of dreams as sources of insight into unconscious desires.

Pages:196

Psychology   ISBN: *1-59462-905-6*   *MSRP $15.45*

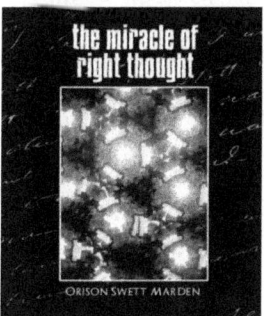

The Miracle of Right Thought
Orison Swett Marden

QTY

Believe with all of your heart that you will do what you were made to do. When the mind has once formed the habit of holding cheerful, happy, prosperous pictures, it will not be easy to form the opposite habit. It does not matter how improbable or how far away this realization may see, or how dark the prospects may be, if we visualize them as best we can, as vividly as possible, hold tenaciously to them and vigorously struggle to attain them, they will gradually become actualized, realized in the life. But a desire, a longing without endeavor, a yearning abandoned or held indifferently will vanish without realization.

Pages:360

Self Help   ISBN: *1-59462-644-8*   *MSRP $25.45*

☐ **The Rosicrucian Cosmo-Conception Mystic Christianity** by *Max Heindel* ISBN: *1-59462-188-8* **$38.95**
The Rosicrucian Cosmo-conception is not dogmatic, neither does it appeal to any other authority than the reason of the student. It is: not controversial, but is: sent forth in the, hope that it may help to clear... New Age/Religion Pages 646

☐ **Abandonment To Divine Providence** by *Jean-Pierre de Caussade* ISBN: *1-59462-228-0* **$25.95**
"The Rev. Jean Pierre de Caussade was one of the most remarkable spiritual writers of the Society of Jesus in France in the 18th Century. His death took place at Toulouse in 1751. His works have gone through many editions and have been republished... Inspirational/Religion Pages 400

☐ **Mental Chemistry** by *Charles Haanel* ISBN: *1-59462-192-6* **$23.95**
Mental Chemistry allows the change of material conditions by combining and appropriately utilizing the power of the mind. Much like applied chemistry creates something new and unique out of careful combinations of chemicals the mastery of mental chemistry... New Age/Business Pages 354

☐ **The Letters of Robert Browning and Elizabeth Barret Barrett 1845-1846 vol II** ISBN: *1-59462-193-4* **$35.95**
by *Robert Browning* and *Elizabeth Barrett*
  Biographies Pages 596

☐ **Gleanings In Genesis (volume I)** by *Arthur W. Pink* ISBN: *1-59462-130-6* **$27.45**
Appropriately has Genesis been termed "the seed plot of the Bible" for in it we have, in germ form, almost all of the great doctrines which are afterwards fully developed in the books of Scripture which follow... Religion/Inspirational Pages 420

☐ **The Master Key** by *L. W. de Laurence* ISBN: *1-59462-001-6* **$30.95**
In no branch of human knowledge has there been a more lively increase of the spirit of research during the past few years than in the study of Psychology, Concentration and Mental Discipline. The requests for authentic lessons in Thought Control, Mental Discipline and... New Age/Business Pages 422

☐ **The Lesser Key Of Solomon Goetia** by *L. W. de Laurence* ISBN: *1-59462-092-X* **$9.95**
This translation of the first book of the "Lernegton" which is now for the first time made accessible to students of Talismanic Magic was done, after careful collation and edition, from numerous Ancient Manuscripts in Hebrew, Latin, and French... New Age/Occult Pages 92

☐ **Rubaiyat Of Omar Khayyam** by *Edward Fitzgerald* ISBN:*1-59462-332-5* **$13.95**
Edward Fitzgerald, whom the world has already learned, in spite of his own efforts to remain within the shadow of anonymity, to look upon as one of the rarest poets of the century, was born at Bredfield, in Suffolk, on the 31st of March, 1809. He was the third son of John Purcell... Music Pages 172

☐ **Ancient Law** by *Henry Maine* ISBN: *1-59462-128-4* **$29.95**
The chief object of the following pages is to indicate some of the earliest ideas of mankind, as they are reflected in Ancient Law, and to point out the relation of those ideas to modern thought. Religiom/History Pages 452

☐ **Far-Away Stories** by *William J. Locke* ISBN: *1-59462-129-2* **$19.45**
"Good wine needs no bush, but a collection of mixed vintages does. And this book is just such a collection. Some of the stories I do not want to remain buried for ever in the museum files of dead magazine-numbers an author's not unpardonable vanity..." Fiction Pages 272

☐ **Life of David Crockett** by *David Crockett* ISBN: *1-59462-250-7* **$27.45**
"Colonel David Crockett was one of the most remarkable men of the times in which he lived. Born in humble life, but gifted with a strong will, an indomitable courage, and unremitting perseverance... Biographies/New Age Pages 424

☐ **Lip-Reading** by *Edward Nitchie* ISBN: *1-59462-206-X* **$25.95**
Edward B. Nitchie, founder of the New York School for the Hard of Hearing, now the Nitchie School of Lip-Reading, Inc, wrote "LIP-READING Principles and Practice". The development and perfecting of this meritorious work on lip-reading was an undertaking... How-to Pages 400

☐ **A Handbook of Suggestive Therapeutics, Applied Hypnotism, Psychic Science** ISBN: *1-59462-214-0* **$24.95**
by *Henry Munro*
  Health/New Age/Health/Self-help Pages 376

☐ **A Doll's House: and Two Other Plays** by *Henrik Ibsen* ISBN: *1-59462-112-8* **$19.95**
Henrik Ibsen created this classic when in revolutionary 1848 Rome. Introducing some striking concepts in playwriting for the realist genre, this play has been studied the world over. Fiction/Classics/Plays 308

☐ **The Light of Asia** by *sir Edwin Arnold* ISBN: *1-59462-204-3* **$13.95**
In this poetic masterpiece, Edwin Arnold describes the life and teachings of Buddha. The man who was to become known as Buddha to the world was born as Prince Gautama of India but he rejected the worldly riches and abandoned the reigns of power when... Religion/History/Biographies Pages 170

☐ **The Complete Works of Guy de Maupassant** by *Guy de Maupassant* ISBN: *1-59462-157-8* **$16.95**
"For days and days, nights and nights, I had dreamed of that first kiss which was to consecrate our engagement, and I knew not on what spot I should put my lips..." Fiction/Classics Pages 240

☐ **The Art of Cross-Examination** by *Francis L. Wellman* ISBN: *1-59462-309-0* **$26.95**
Written by a renowned trial lawyer, Wellman imparts his experience and uses case studies to explain how to use psychology to extract desired information through questioning. How-to/Science/Reference Pages 408

☐ **Answered or Unanswered?** by *Louisa Vaughan* ISBN: *1-59462-248-5* **$10.95**
Miracles of Faith in China
  Religion Pages 112

☐ **The Edinburgh Lectures on Mental Science (1909)** by *Thomas* ISBN: *1-59462-008-3* **$11.95**
This book contains the substance of a course of lectures recently given by the writer in the Queen Street Hall, Edinburgh. Its purpose is to indicate the Natural Principles governing the relation between Mental Action and Material Conditions... New Age/Psychology Pages 148

☐ **Ayesha** by *H. Rider Haggard* ISBN: *1-59462-301-5* **$24.95**
Verily and indeed it is the unexpected that happens! Probably if there was one person upon the earth from whom the Editor of this, and of a certain previous history, did not expect to hear again... Classics Pages 380

☐ **Ayala's Angel** by *Anthony Trollope* ISBN: *1-59462-352-X* **$29.95**
The two girls were both pretty, but Lucy who was twenty-one who supposed to be simple and comparatively unattractive, whereas Ayala was credited, as her Bombwhat romantic name might show, with poetic charm and a taste for romance. Ayala when her father died was nineteen... Fiction Pages 484

☐ **The American Commonwealth** by *James Bryce* ISBN: *1-59462-286-8* **$34.45**
An interpretation of American democratic political theory. It examines political mechanics and society from the perspective of Scotsman James Bryce Politics Pages 572

☐ **Stories of the Pilgrims** by *Margaret P. Pumphrey* ISBN: *1-59462-116-0* **$17.95**
This book explores pilgrims religious oppression in England as well as their escape to Holland and eventual crossing to America on the Mayflower, and their early days in New England... History Pages 268

QTY

The Fasting Cure *by Sinclair Upton*   ISBN: *1-59462-222-1*   **$13.95**
In the Cosmopolitan Magazine for May, 1910, and in the Contemporary Review (London) for April, 1910, I published an article dealing with my experiences in fasting. I have written a great many magazine articles, but never one which attracted so much attention... New Age/Self Help/Health Pages 164

Hebrew Astrology *by Sepharial*   ISBN: *1-59462-308-2*   **$13.45**
In these days of advanced thinking it is a matter of common observation that we have left many of the old landmarks behind and that we are now pressing forward to greater heights and to a wider horizon than that which represented the mind-content of our progenitors... Astrology Pages 144

Thought Vibration or The Law of Attraction in the Thought World   ISBN: *1-59462-127-6*   **$12.95**
by William Walker Atkinson   Psychology/Religion Pages 144

Optimism *by Helen Keller*   ISBN: *1-59462-108-X*   **$15.95**
Helen Keller was blind, deaf, and mute since 19 months old, yet famously learned how to overcome these handicaps, communicate with the world, and spread her lectures promoting optimism. An inspiring read for everyone... Biographies/Inspirational Pages 84

Sara Crewe *by Frances Burnett*   ISBN: *1-59462-360-0*   **$9.45**
In the first place, Miss Minchin lived in London. Her home was a large, dull, tall one, in a large, dull square, where all the houses were alike, and all the sparrows were alike, and where all the door-knockers made the same heavy sound... Childrens/Classic Pages 88

The Autobiography of Benjamin Franklin *by Benjamin Franklin*   ISBN: *1-59462-135-7*   **$24.95**
The Autobiography of Benjamin Franklin has probably been more extensively read than any other American historical work, and no other book of its kind has had such ups and downs of fortune. Franklin lived for many years in England, where he was agent... Biographies/History Pages 332

Name	
Email	
Telephone	
Address	
City, State ZIP	

☐ **Credit Card**   ☐ **Check / Money Order**

Credit Card Number	
Expiration Date	
Signature	

Please Mail to: Book Jungle
PO Box 2226
Champaign, IL 61825
or Fax to: 630-214-0564

ORDERING INFORMATION

web: *www.bookjungle.com*
email: *sales@bookjungle.com*
fax: *630-214-0564*
mail: *Book Jungle PO Box 2226 Champaign, IL 61825*
or PayPal *to sales@bookjungle.com*

Please contact us for bulk discounts

DIRECT-ORDER TERMS

**20% Discount if You Order
Two or More Books**
Free Domestic Shipping!
Accepted: Master Card, Visa,
Discover, American Express

www.ingramcontent.com/pod-product-compliance
Lightning Source LLC
Chambersburg PA
CBHW081232090426
42738CB00016B/3268